Participation in American Politics

PARTICIPATION IN AMERICAN POLITICS

The Dynamics of Agenda-Building

SECOND EDITION

ROGER W. COBB
CHARLES D. ELDER

The Johns Hopkins University Press
Baltimore and London

© Copyright 1972, 1983 by Roger W. Cobb and Charles D. Elder
All rights reserved
Printed in the United States of America
The Johns Hopkins University Press, Baltimore, Maryland 21218
The Johns Hopkins Press Ltd., London

Library of Congress Cataloging in Publication Data

Cobb, Roger W.
Participation in American politics.

Includes index.
1. Political participation—United States.   2. United
States—Politics and government—1945–   3. Social
conflict—United States.   I. Elder, Charles D.
II. Title.
JK1764.C54   1983   323'.042'0973   83–48051
ISBN 0–8018–3086–9 (pbk.)

Dedicated to

DAVID ELDER and EUGENE BERGMAN

who inspired us to seek a better understanding
of the world in which we live.

Contents

Preface to the Second Edition

More than a decade has passed since this book first appeared. We have been gratified by the response it has received. Much has changed however, and were we writing it today, it would undoubtedly be a somewhat different book. Nonetheless, we believe that our basic arguments have stood up rather well and that the framework we suggested remains useful. As a consequence, in this enlarged edition, we have left the original text largely intact and have simply added an epilogue that reflects our current thinking and elaborates on some of our earlier themes.

We remain convinced that agenda-building constitutes a particularly critical phase in the policy process. We also remain convinced that wide-spread participation, either directly or indirectly, in agenda-building is essential to the vitality of a polity that would be democratic. Thus, it is our hope that the enlarged edition will continue to help spur efforts to better understand the dynamics of this vital process.

Preface to the First Edition

This book is designed to introduce the student of politics to a newly developing paradigm for the analysis of political phenomena. In recent years, political inquiry has concentrated on two distinct types of problems. First, it has sought to illuminate and explain the nature of popular participation, especially voting behavior. Second, it has given considerable attention to the dynamics of governmental decision-making. Study in both of these areas has added much to our understanding of American politics. However, it has left a gap, because the processes occurring at the two different levels are seldom linked in any explicit way.

The agenda-building perspective directs our attention to this vital linkage and encourages inquiry into the relationship between mass participation and elite decision-making. It raises important, but largely unexplored, questions that may be critical to the vitality of a democratic polity, suggesting that public participation in political decision-making may extend well beyond the mere selection of the governing elite to selection and resolution of the major issues that a government will confront.

Agenda-building has been touched upon and dealt with peripherally by several major approaches in the study of politics; however, it has remained largely tangential to all of these. We attempt to show how a variety of perspectives impinge upon the problems of agenda-building. The agenda-building paradigm allows us to merge an otherwise disparate range of facts and to synthesize a number of leading approaches.

In developing the framework, we have taken some liberty in interpreting the work of other scholars so as to redirect their insights to the central concern. Nonetheless, in drawing on the works of others, we have tried to remain true to the sense of the authors and to accurately reflect the substance of their arguments that bears upon the agenda-building problem.

We have focused upon the American polity in our effort to delineate the major facets of the agenda-building framework. A wide variety of case study material is provided at the local, state, and national levels to show the generalizability of the model. In limiting our attention to the American system, our intent is not to suggest that the framework is that restricted in its potential applicability. Indeed, it may be relevant in explaining the dynamics of many other political systems. Focus on other systems may lead to greater refinement and elaboration of the general paradigm.

Many of the notions set forth need further development and refinement. It is our hope that the book will spark efforts to develop the framework further through systematic elaboration and rigorous empirical inquiry.

To those who are unfamiliar with our particular style of collaboration, it is difficult to convey the extent to which this book represents a totally joint enterprise. Unlike some collaborative efforts where the authors write different sections, this manuscript was planned and drafted jointly. Therefore, it is impossible to attribute specific authorship to any portion of the book; and we assume responsibility for its insights and errors collectively.

The genesis of the book was sparked in part by Lee F. Anderson, a virtually inexhaustible source of ideas, whose advice and encouragement contributed substantially to its completion. His counsel was typically provocative, and his openness and imagination a prod to our thinking. We also would like to thank Edgar Litt for his comments on an earlier draft of the manuscript. We also are indebted to several anonymous readers who, through the publisher, provided a number of helpful suggestions and criticisms. Finally, we are pleased to acknowledge *The Journal of Politics,* which permitted us to include material that appeared in the November, 1971, issue of the journal under the title "The Politics of Agenda-Building: An Alternative Perspective for Modern Democratic Theory."

Participation in American Politics

1

Agenda-Building
and Democratic Politics

The fall of the Weimar Republic and the rise of Nazi and fascistic movements in the first half of the twentieth century sent out trembles that were to shake the very foundations of democratic thought. As a simple act of faith, democratic theorists had assumed that the common man had both the right and the ability to participate in his own governance. Presumedly, if given the opportunity, the overwhelming majority of people in any polity would be reasonable, relatively rational, and responsible political actors. Hitler's rise to political power in a constitutional system that had been modeled scrupulously to be a showpiece of democracy, coupled with the historically unparalleled rise of mass movements throughout the world, called this traditional democratic faith and trust in the common man into severe question.

Any remaining confidence was to be further rocked, if not destroyed, with the advent of modern empirical research on public opinion and popular participation in those political systems that had long served as models of stable democracy. The classical theory of democracy required that "the electorate possess appropriate personality structures, that it be interested and participate in public affairs, that it be informed, that it be principled, that it correctly perceive political realities, that it engage in discussion, that it judge rationally, and that it consider the community interests." [1] Systematic research over the last two decades consistently revealed that these high standards and historically perceived requisites for democracy were not met or even approached by any western democracy. Studies in the United States, for example, revealed strong strains of authoritarianism, abiding prejudice, and low levels of tolerance in the general population. [2]

Most people tend to exhibit little interest in public affairs, and few participate actively. In fact, in all but national elections, less than a majority even bother to vote. [3] Perhaps that is just as well, given the abominable state of popular knowledge and information about political issues. Even among persons holding political opinions, it has been found that these opinions are often based on little or no factual information or knowledge. Studies of public opinion have further shown that rather than seeking out diverse sources of information, people tend to screen out potentially dissonant information and to perceive political stimuli selectively in terms of preconceived notions. Similarly, if one discusses politics at all, it tends to be with people who are in fundamental agreement with one's views. [4] Thus, the classical assumption of popular competence has been demonstrated to be a myth even in those polities that seemed to have been most successful at democratic government.

That "democratic governments continue to flourish and provide reasonably satisfactory governance for their citizens," [5] despite the fact that the average citizen does not and perhaps cannot play the role that classical theorists would have him play, has presented political science with the problem of reconciling democratic theory with reality. This problem of reformulating democratic theory has been a major preoccupation of a number of theorists over the past two decades and has led to highly heated controversies. The dominant

[1] Bernard Berelson, "Democratic Theory and Public Opinion," *Public Opinion Quarterly* 16 (1952), p. 329.
[2] James Prothro and Charles Grigg, "Fundamental Principles of Democracy: Bases of Agreement and Disagreement," *Journal of Politics* 22 (1960), pp. 276–94; Herbert McClosky, "Consensus and Ideology in American Politics," *American Political Science Review* 58 (1964), pp. 361–82; and Robert Lane, *Political Ideology* (New York: Free Press, 1965).
[3] Lester Milbrath, *Political Participation* (Chicago: Rand McNally & Company, 1965).
[4] Robert Lane and David Sears, *Public Opinion* (Englewood Cliffs, N.J.: Prentice-Hall, 1964).
[5] Milbrath, *op. cit.*, p. 143.

theme emerging from these efforts to reconcile theory and reality has been characterized as *democratic elitism,* or the *elitist theory of democracy.*[6] Here the focus of attention is shifted from political man to a more systemic level, and logical priorities are reversed.

The first question in classical thought of the role of the average citizen in a democracy becomes secondary and dependent, and the primary question becomes, What are the social (not the individual) requisites of stable, effective, and reasonably responsive government? From this perspective, the low levels of interest and participation are seen not as a malady or a blemish, but as a symptom of the basic soundness of the system and positive evidence of an underlying confidence in the government and general satisfaction with the status quo. As Lester Milbrath suggests, "there is doubt that the society as a whole would benefit if intense and active involvement in politics became widespread throughout the population." [7] Thus, widespread, active interest and participation, once seen as a requisite for a stable, effectively functioning democracy, becomes an indicator of a faltering and potentially unstable system. The revised requisites become (1) social pluralism, (2) diverse and competing elites that are circulating and accessible, (3) a basic consensus at least among the elites on the rules of democratic competition, and (4) elections that provide regular opportunities for citizens to participate in the selection of public officials. The discredited fact of government through the active participation of population is not to be discarded, however. It is a myth that is functional for the system. Again quoting Milbrath,

> it is important to continue moral admonishment for citizens to become active in politics, not because we want or expect great masses of them to become active, but rather because the admonishment

[6] Perhaps it would be more appropriate to call the theory one of plu-alistic democratic elitism. For convenience, we will use the term *modern democratic theory*. It is really only a partial theory. Statements of modern democratic theory include Seymour Lipset, *Political Man* (Garden City, N.Y.: Doubleday & Company, 1960); Seymour Lipset, *The First New Nation* (Garden City, N.Y.: Doubleday, 1967); Joseph Schumpeter, *Capitalism, Socialism and Democracy* (New York: Harper & Row, Publishers, 1942); V. O. Key, *The Responsible Electorate* (Cambridge: Belknap Press of Harvard University Press, 1966); Robert Dahl, *A Preface to Democratic Theory* (Chicago: University of Chicago Press, 1956); Robert Dahl, *Who Governs?* (New Haven: Yale University Press, 1961); and V. O. Key, *Public Opinion and American Democracy* (New York: Alfred A. Knopf, 1961).

[7] Milbrath, *op. cit.,* p. 147.

helps keep the system open and sustains the belief in the right of all to participate, which is an important norm governing the behavior of political elites.[8]

There can be no doubt that the revised theory of democracy is empirically more viable as a descriptive statement of functioning democracies than classical theory. By focusing at the systems level, the revised theory can reasonably explain phenomena that must be regarded as anomalies in classical theory. In fact, from the systemic point of view, it is possible to demonstrate in a fairly compelling fashion that the often irrationally based and ill-informed decisions of individual voters add up to a highly rational and responsible collective choice.[9]

Systems of Limited Participation

As the revised theory has increasingly assumed the status of the conventional wisdom, the type and range of major questions upon which attention is concentrated has changed. Questions of stability, characteristics of elites, and internal governmental decision-making become paramount. Classical questions about the distribution of influence, equality of access, individual freedom and self-actualization through political participation become less salient. However, even the most sanguine interpretations of existing democracies by contemporary democratic theorists admit that control and access is unevenly distributed in the population. As Robert Dahl writes:

> I do not know how to quantify this control, but if it could be quantified I suppose it would be no exaggeration to say that Mr. Henry Luce has a thousand or ten thousand times greater control over the alternatives scheduled for debate and tentative decision at a national election than I do. . . . It is a reasonable preliminary hypothesis that the number of individuals who exercise significant control over the alternatives scheduled is . . . only a tiny fraction of the total membership.[10]

[8] *Ibid.*, p. 152.
[9] V. O. Key, *The Responsible Electorate,* passim.
[10] Robert Dahl, *Preface to Democratic Theory,* pp. 72–73.

Despite this acknowledgment, most contemporary theorists have exhibited relatively little formal concern with the scope of participation and influence in the determination of political decisional alternatives. They concentrate on those who do influence key decisions and how. Yet Schattschneider admonishes us that narrow participation in the selection of political alternatives will reinforce existing bias in the direction of the polity and undermine its long run stability.[11] He contends that participation in the arena of conflict where political alternatives are determined is highly restricted. Referring to this arena as the pressure system, he characterizes it as "essentially the politics of small groups." He notes that "the flaw in the pluralist heaven is that the heavenly chorus sings with a strong upper class accent. Probably 90 percent of the population cannot get into the pressure system." [12]

The pressure system is thus limited to "legitimate" groups, which includes only those that have already gained access to the political arena. Entry into the pressure system for previously excluded groups may require extralegal action or behavior that is outside the legitimate "rules of the game." Gamson writes:

> the American political system normally operates to prevent incipient competitors from achieving full entry into the political arena. Far from there being built-in mechanisms which keep the system responsive, such groups win entry only through the breakdown of the normal operation of the system or through demonstration on the part of challenging groups of a willingness to violate the "rules of the game" by resorting to illegitimate means.[13]

This greatly restricts the types of issues and conflicts that can develop over scarcities in the system. Those who have the greatest needs are ordinarily not included in the pressure system, and it is imbalanced in terms of accurately reflecting the basic conflicts throughout society. Gamson notes:

> This results in a situation in which large numbers of citizens are outside the political arena in which competition and influence

---

[11] E. E. Schattschneider, *The Semi-Sovereign People* (New York: Holt, Rinehart and Winston, 1960).

[12] *Ibid.,* p. 35.

[13] William Gamson, "Stable Unrepresentation in American Society," *American Behavioral Scientist* 12 (November–December, 1968), p. 18.

occur. . . . This situation can be described as one of stable unrepresentation . . . [and] the normal operation of the political system serves to amplify the power of those groups which already possess it.[14]

Stable unrepresentation suggests a bias in terms of the issues
and demands that will be considered in a political system and raises
important, but largely unexamined, questions about ways in which issues are selected and resolved in a polity. Thus, the question of the
distribution of influence is raised again, but now the question is not
one relating to the influence over decisions, but rather influence over
the range and types of alternatives considered.

Reactions to Systems of Limited Participation

While the revised theory of democracy serves to resolve one intellectual crisis (viz., that of reconciling theory with reality), it has created
another, a threefold crisis that has practical as well as intellectual implications. The first aspect of this crisis may be called a *prescriptive
crisis*. Classical democratic theory sought to serve as both a descriptive statement and a normative prescription. As a normative theory,
it provided a goal with relatively clear-cut criteria for evaluating
progress towards it. Most contemporary theorists would not contend
that their theory is any more than descriptive. Nonetheless, the theory
undermines the very criteria that gave classical theory its potency as a
normative goal. Insofar as modern democratic thought has replaced
classical theory, there is a danger that it too will be elevated to serve
a normative as well as a descriptive function. Because the modern
theory of democracy was developed only as descriptive theory, it perhaps "unwittingly purveys an ideology of social conservatism tem-
pered by modest incremental change." [15] In other words, taking it as
the basis for new evaluative criteria carries with it a strongly conservative bias.

By revising the theory to bring it into closer correspondence with
reality, the elitist theorists have transformed democracy from a rad-

[14] *Ibid.,* p. 19.
[15] David Easton, "The New Revolution in Political Science," *American Political Science Review* 63 (1969), p. 1052.

ical into a conservative political doctrine, stripping away its distinctive emphasis on popular political activity so that it no longer serves as a set of ideals toward which society ought to be striving.[16]

Thus, the theory can become little more than a rationalization for the status quo. In shifting the focus away from the individual and popular participation and to the systemic level, the theory certainly invites at least the implicit introduction of new evaluative criteria or goals; namely, those of stability and efficiency. Thus, "on its face it would appear that the democrat is left with a Hobson's choice: a theory which is normatively sound but unrealistic, or a theory which is realistic but heavily skewed toward elitism." [17]

The second problem with the modern theory of democracy is related to the first and may be called a *crisis of relevance*. Because the theory simply describes existing systems and provides a macro-level explanation of the normal functions of the conventional political machinery of these systems, it provides no guidelines for social change or direction for political action. By concentrating on "the maintenance of democratic stability, the preservation of democratic procedures, and the creation of machinery which would produce efficient administration and coherent policies," [18] it forces major social conflicts and social movements to be viewed more as aberrations than a normal part of political life. This viewpoint does not "help political science reach out to the real needs of mankind in a time of crisis." [19] The theory provides neither the knowledge nor the perspective to implement remedial social action. Dramatic innovation, mobilization, and violence are the frequent companions of social change even in democratic systems. It is insufficient to regard these as simply disruptive influences or precipitants of crises in the normal operations of democracy. Ironically, in a time when all of these problems loom large and cry out for resolution, our revised theory of democracy offers no guidance.

To the protesting students throughout the world who are saying "the existing system—the power structure—is hypocritical, unwor-

---

[16] Jack Walker, "A Critique of the Elitist Theory of Democracy," *American Political Science Review* 60 (1966), p. 288.
[17] Peter Bachrach, *The Theory of Democratic Elitism: A Critique* (Boston: Little, Brown and Company, 1967), p. 99.
[18] Walker, *op. cit.*, p. 293.
[19] Easton, *op. cit.*, p. 1052.

thy of respect, outmoded, and in urgent need of reform," who "speak of repression, manipulation and authoritarianism," and who complain "about being suffocated by the subtle tyranny of the Establishment," [20] the theory says nothing and even fails to recognize their concerns. At a time when students, blacks, and other minority groups are revolting against centralized power and demanding full participation—"not merely the consent of the governed but the involvement of the governed" [21]—modern theorists suggest that *participatory democracy* is an anathema to stable democratic government and by default seemingly accept stable unrepresentation or underrepresentation as a natural, if not necessary, condition. To urgent questions such as How can the priorities of a democratic system be altered or changed? How can it be mobilized to meet the pressing demands of a decaying environment, overpopulation, and the need for full recognition and acceptance of the civil rights of all men? the theory is silent in content and largely devoid of relevant inferences.

The third major aspect of the general crisis of democratic theory is closely related to the second and may be called a *crisis of research guidance*. As a research paradigm, modern theory directs attention to an important and perhaps insufficiently examined range of phenomena. In so doing, however, it tends to dictate research priorities and prescribe both the type and range of phenomena considered. It is not that the questions it leads us to ask are unimportant, but rather that other important questions tend not to be explored. For example, it leads us to ask what function different levels of participation have for the system, but not the functions participation may have for the individual. It leads us to explore the exercise of power in decision-making situations, but to overlook "the equally, if not more important area of what . . . [may be] called nondecision-making, that is, the practice of limiting the scope of actual decision-making to 'safe' issues by manipulating the dominant community values, myths, and political institutions and procedures." [22] It directs our attention to the consensual basis of conflict management and the incremental character of normal political decision-making, but it ig-

[20] Kenneth Keniston, "You Have to Grow Up in Scarsdale to Know How Bad Things Really Are," *The New York Times Magazine,* April 27, 1969, p. 127.
[21] *Ibid.,* p. 130.
[22] Peter Bachrach and Morton Baratz, *Power and Poverty* (New York: Oxford University Press, 1970), p. 18.

nores or treats as an aberrant condition violence and the threat of violence. Both can be important political resources for spurring social change even in a relatively stable democratic system.

While modern theory directs our attention to the ubiquitous and omnipresent nature of elites and their critical role in the direction of a polity, it fails to specify the points in the system and conditions under which the masses may participate in the shaping and determination of major policy issues. Consequently, contemporary political science perspectives are unable to cope with or explain how a previously dormant issue can be transformed into a highly salient political controversy at a specific point when the basis of the grievance has existed for some time; for example, the pollution problem.

An Alternative Perspective

The inevitable biases in the revised theory of democracy have provoked several scholars to react to the crises discussed above. For example, Bachrach has attempted to speak to the prescriptive vacuum created by the debunking of classical democratic theory. By extending the scope of applicability of political norms to all sectors of society where authoritative decisions are made regarding the allocation of values significant to the society, he has attempted to revitalize and give new meaning to the norm of participation and to reassert the social and individual value of active involvement of individuals in the processes that affect their lives.[23] The so-called post-behavioralist or neo-traditionalist movement represents a response to the crisis of relevance.[24] Here the emphasis is on attempting to address major contemporary problems as systematically as possible, providing the best available guidance for social change despite the absence of complete knowledge. Perhaps the most significant response has come with respect to the crisis of research guidance. It is this response that provided a major impetus for the development of the arguments presented in this book.

The response is predicated on four fairly elementary observa-

[23] Bachrach, *Theory of Democratic Elitism,* passim.
[24] See, for example, Easton, *op. cit.,* pp. 1051–61; or Michael Haas and Henry Kariel (eds.), *Approaches to the Study of Political Science* (San Francisco: Chandler Publishing Company, 1970).

tions that most modern democratic theorists acknowledge but tend not to develop. First, the distribution of influence and access in any system has inherent biases. Consequently, the system will operate to the favor of some and to the disadvantage of others. As Dahl observes,

> in all human organizations there are significant variations in the participation in political decisions—variations which in the United States appear to be functionally related to such variables as concern or involvement, skill, access, socio-economic status, education, residence, age, ethnic and religious identifications, and some little understood personality characteristics.[25]

The second observation follows from the first and notes that the range of issues and decisional alternatives that will be considered by a polity is restricted. This restriction arises from two sources. The first is a systems imperative and is predicated on the fact that the processing and attention capabilities of any human organization are necessarily limited. The second source of restriction arises from the fact that "all forms of political organization have a bias in favor of the exploitation of some kinds of conflict and the suppression of others because *organization is the mobilization of bias.* Some issues are organized into politics while others are organized out." [26]

Since the existing bias of a political system both reflects and legitimizes the prevailing balance of power among organized groups, it follows that the range and type of issues and alternatives considered will represent the interests and most salient concerns of previously legitimized political forces. Assuming that the popular balance of forces is subject to change, priorities in the system in terms of issues and alternatives will always be out of step with the ongoing struggle for influence; and thus, old issues will always tend to command the most prominent positions in formal political deliberations.

Flowing from the above, the third observation is that the system's inertia makes it extremely difficult to change the prevailing bias in terms of the types of issues and alternatives that are not only considered but also viewed as legitimate concerns of the polity. As Walker has observed: "The agenda of controversy, the list of ques-

[25] Dahl, *Preface to Democratic Theory,* pp. 71–72.
[26] Schattschneider, *op. cit.,* p. 71.

tions which are recognized by the active participants in politics as legitimate subjects of attention and concern, is very hard to change." [27] Thus, there is a strong status quo bias in any existing system, and the legal machinery of that system is designed and operates to reinforce and defend that bias.

> Power groups of the status quo may use legality and the police to maintain privileges and social norms that no longer reflect the real bargaining relations among groups. This is especially likely when their legitimate social assets are weakening and when their interests are undergoing serious challenge. . . . Whoever is advantaged by the law in his bargaining relationships with others will seek to maintain a doctrine of legality; he will assert the automatic enforceability of "the letter of the law" and may seek to buttress some laws by new laws which narrow or foreclose the gambits of future discretion.[28]

The contemporary commonplace appeal for "law and order" may then be seen not only as reflecting a desire for peace, stability, and predictability but also, and perhaps more importantly, as a bargaining ploy to protect the advantage of previously legitimized interests. Understandably, then, established interests may be willing to change and to consider previously excluded issues and demands only under the threat of severe disruption of the status quo. To make such a threat both credible and visible, underrepresented or unrepresented groups may have to demonstrate willingness to use extralegal or even illegal means, such as resorting to violence. As Bachrach and Baratz observe:

> Subordinate groups, because of their insufficient power resources in relationship to the restrictive political system, are often unable to convert their demands for change into important political issues. As their grievances grow . . . such groups not uncommonly back their demands by the threat of violence or by actual violence." [29]

The likelihood of success in such outbursts is not high and might even result in a repressive response from the affected decision-mak-

[27] Walker, *op. cit.*, p. 292.
[28] H. L. Nieburg, "Violence, law, and the informal polity," *Journal of Conflict Resolution* 13 (1969), p. 200.
[29] Bachrach and Baratz, *op. cit.*, p. 105.

ers. However, it is one of the few resources that deprived groups can utilize, lacking other means of system access. As Walker has noted: "Through such [violent] trials, as tumultuous as they may be, the agenda of controversy, the list of acceptable, 'key' issues may be changed." [30]

The fourth and final observation is simply a recognition flowing from the first three observations; namely that, pre-political, or at least pre-decisional processes often play the most critical role in determining what issues and alternatives are to be considered by the polity and the probable choices that will be made. What happens in the decision-making councils of the formal institutions of government may do little more than recognize, document, and legalize, if not legitimize, the momentary results of a continuing struggle of forces in the larger social matrix. Thus, to understand the dynamics of democracy, it is necessary to consider what Nieburg calls the *"informal polity,* which underlies and gives vitality to the formal institutions of the social process." [31] From this perspective, the critical question becomes, How does an issue or a demand become or fail to become the focus of concern and interest within a polity? In other words, How does an issue come to be viewed as an important and appropriate subject of attention? How does it come to command a position on the agenda of legitimate political controversy? or How is it denied this status? Clearly, agenda status is attained through a fairly elaborate process and will not necessarily result from any single decision or action. In fact, the fate of an issue may hinge as much on "nondecisions" as on formal decision-making. Nondecision-making has been described as the process "by which demands for change in the existing allocation of benefits and privileges in a community can be suffocated before they are even voiced; or kept covert; or killed before they gain access to the relevant decisionmaking arena." [32]

Through the manipulation of bias and prevailing values, status quo powers may stifle, reinterpret, or otherwise defuse an issue and thus prevent it from gaining agenda status. Clearly, an advantaged group is tactically remiss if it fails to seek minimal accommodation within the acceptable bounds of its interests with issues that are

[30] Walker, *op. cit.,* p. 294.
[31] Nieburg, *op. cit.,* p. 196.
[32] Bachrach and Baratz, *op. cit.,* p. 44.

likely to become agenda items on their own, otherwise. Thus, under normal circumstances, prevailing social forces will follow something like the "rule of anticipated reaction," [33] claiming the right to interpret the demands of subordinate groups, and acting accordingly. The effect is to deny the subordinate group full entry into the pressure system by denying the basis of a claim to legitimacy, preserving the general content of and control over the existing agenda. In the words of Walker, "It is this constellation of influences and anticipated reactions, 'the peculiar mobilization of bias' in the community, fortified by a general consensus of elites, that determines the agenda of controversy." [34]

There is a growing awareness on the part of deprived groups concerning the importance of crystallizing their objectives into clear proposals so that they can claim agenda status. Indeed, in the civil rights movement, some have realized that entrance onto an agenda is a prerequisite for any type of ameliorative action. This can be noted in the following appeal:

> Dr. Martin Luther King, Jr. once said, "I have a dream," but today he is history. Black students today will not come to you and say "We have a dream." We have an agenda. At the top of our agenda is an end to racism and its immediate manifestation, white skin privilege.[35]

Given the overwhelming importance of such problems in the contemporary world, it is imperative for political science to develop a series of perspectives that can deal more adequately with the above set of phenomena in some type of meaningful context. One such outlet is to focus on the notion of agenda, as alluded to earlier by other analysts. A perspective could then be developed that focuses on the ways in which groups articulate grievances and transform them into viable issues that require decision-makers to provide some type of ameliorative response. It is essentially this problem that we wish to address in the remainder of the book.

[33] Carl Friedrich, *Constitutional Government and Democracy* (Boston: Ginn and Company, 1946), pp. 589–90.
[34] Walker, *op. cit.*, p. 292.
[35] David Anderson, Philip Parkman, Ardina Seward, and Robert Scott, "An Agenda for Involvement," *The MBA* 4, No. 7 (April–May, 1970), p. 34.

The Politics of Agenda-Building

In its most elementary form, the basic question we are raising is, Where do public policy issues come from? We are concerned with how issues are created and why some controversies or incipient issues come to command the attention and concern of the formal centers of decision-making, while others fail. In other words, What are the determinants of the agenda for political controversy within a community? How is an agenda built (i.e., How does an issue gain access to it?)? and Who participates in this process?

Assuming that the balance of social forces influencing, if not controlling, the content of the political agenda at any point in time is necessarily biased to the advantage of some and the disadvantage of others, how may this balance be changed, and with what consequences? It should be noted that we have used the term *agenda* at this point to refer to a general set of political controversies that will be viewed at any point in time as falling within the range of legitimate concerns meriting the attention of the polity.

This, of course, is only one meaning of the term. It may also be used to denote a set of concrete, specific items scheduled for active and serious consideration by a particular institutional decision-making body. Examples would be legislative calendars and the docket of a court. We shall consider institutional agendas as well as what may be called the systemic agenda for political controversy. Of primary concern throughout will be the relationship between the two types of agendas.

The systemic agenda will always be more abstract, general, and broader in scope and domain than any given institutional agenda. Moreover, the priorities in this systemic agenda will not necessarily correspond with the priorities in institutional agendas. In fact, there may be considerable discrepancy between them. It may be offered as a general hypothesis that the greater the disparity between the two types of agendas, the greater the intensity and frequency of conflict within the political system.

Because of the inertia present in any system, institutional agendas will always lag to some extent behind the more general systemic agenda. Among other things, this means that there will be a modicum of social conflict in even the most responsive system. The extent of this lag will be magnified in periods of severe system discontinuities such as depression, war, and technological change. If the lag becomes too great, the system will stop functioning effectively and may even be destroyed. A corollary of our earlier proposition would be that the viability of a polity is a direct function of its ability to cope with the problem of lag between the two types of agendas and to keep the magnitude of the lag within tolerable limits. This arises from the fact that legitimacy, unlike legality, is always conditional and must be earned and sustained if the system is to retain popular confidence and its vitality.

To further develop and deal with the questions raised above, we will want to consider a wide range of phenomena and a variety of approaches to the study of politics. For example, we will examine processes of participation, mobilization, and media participation. Succeeding chapters will provide insights into the problem of agenda-building in terms of major theoretical frameworks developed in political science. We will try to outline the major features of conflict that bear on issue creation and development and to review the relevant literature on the dynamics of issue conflict. We shall also consider symbolic aspects of the agenda-building process and explore the ways that different symbols are used to redefine issue conflicts so as to disadvantage the competition.

We shall also address ourselves to the specific questions of what constitutes an agenda and where it is located, as well as what constitutes an issue and what the relevant events or mechanisms are that trigger issues. Issues will be considered in terms of certain key characteristics to include their audience or publics. A framework will be developed for investigating how different issues become relevant to various types of publics. In this context, a series of propositions will be advanced that link the intensity and extensity of popular involvement to certain key issue characteristics. An effort will be made to delineate the major channels by which issues are transformed into items on a public docket. In the process of showing how the characteristics of issues and the expansion of popular participation relate to the agenda-building process, we hope to provide at least the outlines of an integrated approach to the study of how issues gain agenda access.

To treat all of these problems adequately involves isolating relevant factors and interrelating them systematically. Analysis must be conducted across levels (that is, at all governmental levels), and consideration must be given to numerous units. It is not surprising to find a number of existing social science research paradigms or approaches to the study of political phenomena of potential relevance. In fact, by focusing on the problems of agenda-building and issue access, we are perhaps afforded a perspective that will facilitate the synthesis and integration of a diverse range of phenomena.

In the following chapter, the problems of agenda-building will be assayed in the context of four leading approaches to the study of politics. Each will serve to illuminate different facets of the problem and provide insights into its major dimensions. The four analytic frameworks to be examined are systems theory, power analysis, decision-making schema, and the group approach.

Conclusion

A considerable portion of modern political inquiry has been devoted to the problem of reconciling classical theory with empirical reality. Emerging from these efforts is considerable knowledge about the nature of popular participation and the requisites of stable and effective political institutions. That the conditions identified for stable, responsive government obtain cannot be denied. However, contemporary theory tells us little about how these conditions are attained and sustained over time.

In response to this gap in our theoretical understanding and the need to speak to pressing contemporary problems, the elements of a fledgling theory have begun to appear. Utilizing notions that have been traditionally viewed as pre-decisional if not pre-political, we have attempted to show how a constellation of social forces will shape the concerns of a polity and bear on its ultimate vitality. To integrate the diverse elements that appear to be of consequence, it has been useful to focus on the institutional and systemic agendas that prescribe the range of legitimate concerns of the society and prescribe those issues that will command the active attention of political decision-makers. In the ensuing chapters, a framework will be developed and elaborated that draws upon and interrelates major contemporary approaches to illuminate the dynamics of the agenda-building process.

2

The Problem of Agenda-Building
in Past Political Inquiry:
The Confluence of Four Approaches

Past research within the context of political science has focused on the problem of agenda-building by linking general social processes and governmental decision-making. It is generally agreed that social processes (that is, extra-governmental, though not necessarily non-governmental processes) in large measure provide the primordial stuff of political decision-making. The question is how these elements interrelate. To understand how, one must necessarily inquire into the determinants of political agendas.

Let us briefly examine some of the perspectives developed in the social sciences that seem most relevant. This examination will underline the importance of the problems of issue creation and access, and it will provide a convenient starting point for our analysis. We will consider those approaches centering around the concepts of (1) system, (2) power, (3) decision-making, and (4) interest groups or groupings.[1] Later we will give considerably more detailed consideration to the concept of conflict. However, as that will serve as a basis for organizing the analysis, it seems appropriate not to anticipate that discussion.

[1] The more general heading of "grouping" is added to cover those aggregations that might not qualify as interest groups, such as makeshift coalitions in a particular institutional body.

The intent in looking at these four approaches is not to provide anything remotely resembling a comprehensive description; our focus is to show the confluence of the four approaches around the problems of agenda creation in general and issue access in particular.

General Systems Approach

The work of a number of contemporary systems theorists is potentially useful in conceptualizing the ways in which governmental decision-making is linked to general social processes.

SEMINAL WORKS ON SYSTEMS.   The genesis of contemporary systems research that raised, at least peripherally, problems of agenda-building can be traced to the works of David Easton.[2] In a long range project, of which three major works have now been published, Easton has addressed himself to the problems of political analysis from a systems perspective.[3] The political system is seen as one of several subsystems that collectively form an overall social system. The prime function of the political system vis-a-vis the larger system is the "authoritative allocation of valued things." [4]

For our purposes, Easton's third volume, *A Systems Analysis of Political Life,* is particularly instructive. Here Easton attempts to clarify the nature of the inputs into the political system and tries to spell out the mechanisms by means of which these inputs get into the system. Of his two types of inputs (demands and supports), we are

---

[2] This is not to indicate that only the works of David Easton are considered to be seminal contributions to an evaluation of systems approaches. Other works which the reader might consider are Talcott Parsons, *The Social System* (Glencoe: Free Press, 1951); Talcott Parsons and Edward Shils (eds.), *Toward A General Theory of Action* (New York: Harper, 1951); Gabriel Almond, Chapter 1 in Almond and James Coleman (eds.), *The Politics of the Developing Areas* (Princeton: Princeton University Press, 1960); Karl Deutsch, *The Nerves of Government* (New York: Free Press, 1963); Hans Gerth and C. Wright Mills, *Character and Social Structure* (New York: Harcourt, Brace & World, 1953); and Walter Buckeley, *Sociology and Modern Systems Theory* (Englewood Cliffs: Prentice-Hall, 1967).

[3] David Easton, *The Political System* (New York: Knopf, 1953); *A Framework for Political Analysis* (Englewood Cliffs: Prentice-Hall, 1965); and David Easton, *A Systems Analysis of Political Life* (New York: John Wiley & Sons, 1965).

[4] Easton, *Framework for Political Analysis,* p. 50.

primarily interested in demands. As he writes, "Demands may be conceived as a central variable for the simple fact that without them, there would literally be no occasion to undertake the making of binding decisions for a society." [5]

Demands are generated from wants through a process of politicization. That is to say, a want is converted to a demand when an authoritative decision is called for with respect to that want.[6] This does not mean, however, that a demand will necessarily command attention of the systemic agenda or any particular formal agenda.[7] In fact, it is unlikely that many demands will ever go beyond the boundaries of the political system. One important way in which a demand may gain attention and command a place on the agenda of authoritative decision-makers is through the process of conversion to an issue.[8] The conversion of a demand into an issue serves to increase the visibility of the demand and tends to mobilize persons or groups not previously involved, thus giving greater weight to the demand. In other words, the conversion of a demand into an issue essentially means elevating the demand to systemic agenda status. In the process counter-demands will also be activated. All of this activity occurs at various points bounding the political system and subsystems within it.

Generically, Easton calls the process by which demands and issues enter or fail to enter the political system or any of its subsystems "gatekeeping." [9] Those persons, institutions, and groups whose actions determine the success or failure of a demand or issue entering into the system or any of its subsystems are termed "gatekeepers." They not only serve as vehicles for entry into the political system, but also reduce the overall "load" on the system by selectively restricting its inputs and withinputs. Thus, gatekeepers are key participants in the continuous process of agenda-building.

Oran Young also identifies the gatekeeping role as a pivotal one in any political system. He writes as follows:

[5] Easton, *Systems Analysis of Political Life,* p. 48.

[6] *Ibid.,* pp. 80–96.

[7] Note we are using the terms *governmental agenda, institutional agenda* and *formal agenda* as synonyms. The term *political agenda* is used to subsume both systemic and institutional agendas. This usage will continue throughout the book.

[8] Easton, *Systems Analysis of Political Life,* pp. 143–45.

[9] *Ibid.,* pp. 133–37.

Demands can be regulated by various reduction processes. . . . Specific procedures included here are . . . intrasystem gate-keeping procedures and the requirement that general systems demands be converted into specific issues for purposes of political processing.[10]

AN EMPIRICAL APPLICATION.   One of the problems of most of the writings on general systems is that the problem of agendas is identified, but it is not considered important enough to be elaborated in their scheme. While adaptation or lack of it at the systemic level is a prime concern, few articulate the problem in terms of the types of demands that are recognized and filtered.

William Mitchell has been one of the few political scientists writing from a systems perspective who have attempted to conceptualize the demand context more clearly. Mitchell argues that the crystallization of demands into relevant issues confronting the government is one of the most important processes in the political system. He says one must study the intensity of demands, implying that conviction of adherents and the number sharing a belief are important components in terms of achieving agenda access. Other relevant considerations are the extent to which the demands are filtered through intermediate institutions such as the mass media and the number of group resolutions that reflect a particular interest.

Mitchell distinguishes between desires that he calls "expectations" and desires that are translated into overt behavior that he calls "demands." He argues that many expectations never become demands simply because most people have vague, inconsistent, and antithetical views on relevant issues. Most institutional agendas are limited to a small number of items. However, if one views as demands all the bills introduced in Congress each year, the number becomes so great that the agenda must differentiate among existing items, since 20,000 bills per year is simply too many to be dealt with by national decision-makers.

Mitchell argues that institutional agendas have a variety of locations. One simply cannot limit the institutional agenda to a list of

---

[10] Oran Young, *Systems of Political Science* (Englewood Cliffs: Prentice-Hall, 1968), pp. 40–41. For Young's other publications on the utility of general systems approaches in political inquiry, see "The Impact of General Systems Theory on Political Science," *General Systems* 9 (1964), 239–53; and "A Survey of General Systems Theory," *General Systems* 9 (1964), 61–80.

legislative proposals or even to the bills actually being considered by the legislature. Since the American political process is decentralized and has a number of access points, the courts, administrative agencies and cabinet divisions all develop relevant agendas. While the number of demands have increased, they have also become more diversified, with governmental budgets now covering a greater variety of items than ever before.

A utilization of the concept of demands in a systems context also requires knowledge of the stimuli that produce demands within a system. While the available resources for mobilization within a system are scarce, the principal condition leading to an acceleration or a change in the composition of demands is a system dislocation. The sources of dislocation can be found in various sectors of the political system from the economic sector to educational institutions.

Mitchell argues that one of the distinctive features of the American political system is that most people believe they have opportunities for expressing views and believe they have a right to make demands. However, resources are unequally distributed, with advantages given to those with wealth, social status, or a strategic position within the system structure. The system will not retain its viability unless there are able decision-makers who can make institutional agendas that reflect major grievances facing the society at any point in time.

The two principal means of expressing demands in a system are institutionalized vehicles such as elections and noninstitutionalized means such as violence. Mitchell maintains that the former is highly discriminatory in terms of what gains access to governmental agendas because only a certain percentage of the population participates. The interests of that group are reflected by decision-makers in placing items on the docket for consideration. Even so, the American system allows a great deal of latitude in policy selection by elected leaders, so the selection of issues to be included on formal agendas are not directly funneled through the election process. In fact, politicians are the "major articulates on policy matters." [11]

Noninstitutional means such as violence have also been used in the past to place issues on governmental agendas. Entry is gained through first commanding attention on the systemic agenda. Such actions are usually taken when participants believe that they cannot

[11] William Mitchell, *The American Polity* (New York: Free Press, 1962), p. 284.

gain access without recourse to extralegal means. Often, the threat of violence can be even more successful in sustaining the attention of officials than the actual use of violence.[12] However, Mitchell asserts that institutional means are much more common, since the system could not survive continued outbreaks of violent action. In addition, most people are socialized to accept legal statements of limited or moderate demands.[13]

Thus, we can clearly see that the locus of the problems of political agenda-building is essentially those processes occurring at the boundaries of the system and its subsystems. It is here that the social processes operative in the larger environment impinge upon the agenda and mold its concerns. Although the problems of issue access and agenda composition were not vital concerns in the inceptions of the systems models, it has become a topic of increased attention with the passage of time, particularly in terms of the composition of the American system.

The "Power" Approach

Power has long been a central concept in political analysis. Some theorists, in fact, would contend that the study of politics is essentially the study of power. The concept itself is broad and somewhat nebulous.

THE COMPONENTS OF POWER.   Clearly, however, power is a relational concept. That is, its referent is not a concrete attribute or aggregate of characteristics but is rather the character of a particular type of relationship between entities. Specific attributes become relevant only in a relational context. Power is a relationship in which one person has the ability to affect, modify, or in some way shape the actions of another. This ability may arise from the relative character or nature of the units, the situation, or the context. All the concepts subsumable under or synonymous with power (i.e., control, influence, authority) seem to be characterized by this basic relational

[12] For example, see H. L. Nieburg, "The Threat of Violence and Social Change," *American Political Science Review* 56 (1962), 865–73.
[13] Relevant materials that refer to the problem of agenda-building within a political system can be found in Mitchell, *op. cit.*, pp. 13–15; 272–86.

property and are distinguishable, if at all, by the particular circumstances giving rise to this relationship.

It is not surprising that much controversy within and about American politics has centered around questions of power. Nor is it astonishing that political inquiry has focused on mapping power relationships. It is interesting to note the sort of power relations that have commanded the most attention. Without attempting to survey the relevant literature, it seems fair to say that the greatest concern has been direct expressions of power, or manifest power relations.

According to Jack Nagel, there are two important types of power relationships that have been overlooked by most power theorists. The first is the situation of anticipated reaction, and the second is information manipulation. A has power over B to the extent to which he can control the information communicated to B about a particular item. Nagel argues that both of the above fall under the heading of *power* not *persuasion* because if A can persuade B to do x, he has power over B.[14]

Thus, an overt attempt by A to influence B is not required for a power relationship between A and B. Key elements can be the mobilization of bias and the manipulation of subjective factors such as perceptions.

TYPES OF POWER RELATIONSHIPS IN COMMUNITY CONTEXTS. Over the past decades, a conflict has existed between those who wish to study power in a visible context and those who examine the phenomenon in a non-visible context. Recently there has been a dialogue devoted to a possible switch in the study of power from focusing on decisions to examining issues that never reach the attention of decision-makers. Within the context of community power studies, political scientists have been investigating how institutional agendas are developed and who the key individuals are in determining the composition of a docket. *Elitists* argue that a particular group from the community decides which items shall receive attention from local governmental bodies. The *pluralists* have asserted that the local governmental agenda is multi-faceted and is determined by a variety of groups within the community. On a set of issues, one set of groups

---

[14] Jack Nagel, "Some Questions About the Concept of Power," *Behavioral Science* 13 (1968), p. 130.

will have the dominant role, while another set of groups will come to play on a different set of issues. In his study of New Haven, Dahl found that the issue determined who would be involved and that all income groups would have some influence in determining which issues would receive attention from the local government.[15]

Bachrach and Baratz have criticized the pluralist focus on studying power as reflected in a series of overt decisions made by various governing boards. They argue that greater attention must be given to the study of situations when "A devotes his energies to creating or reinforcing social and political values and institutional practices that limit the scope of the political process to public consideration of only those issues which are comparatively innocuous to A." [16] To the extent that A is successful, he can preclude any issue from receiving attention that would be detrimental to his interests. Some researchers have assumed that because certain issues are by reputation the major issues in a community, it necessarily follows that they are the key issues in the community. Bachrach and Baratz argue that this type of thinking unnecessarily restricts the type of research to be done on agenda-building. They argue that the "nondecision" may be more important than the "decision."

In the study of the nondecision, they asserted that existing community values and mores preclude certain types of issues from gaining access to institutional agendas and that it might be more useful to study this process than actual decisions about what resources to allocate where in the public arena.[17]

---

[15] Robert Dahl, *Who Governs?* (New Haven: Yale University Press, 1961)

[16] Peter Bachrach and Morton Baratz, "Two Faces of Power," *American Political Science Review* 56 (1962), p. 948.

[17] The review of certain contentious issues in the study of community power is by no means exhaustive, nor is it intended to be. Our focus here is solely to review those issues in the dispute which are relevant in the study of how disputes gain access to the governmental agenda. Relevant articles on the nondecisionmaking approach are: *Ibid.,* pp. 947–52; and Peter Bachrach and Morton Baratz, "Decisions and Nondecisions: An Analytical Framework," *American Political Science Review* 57 (1963), pp. 632–42. A recent article that makes a critical evaluation of the notions of nondecision-making is Richard Merelman. "On the Neo-Elitist Critique of Community Power," *American Political Science Review* 62 (1968), pp. 451–60. The Bachrach-Baratz notions could have been put under either the "Power" or the "Decision-making" section. Even though they use terms like *decision* and *nondecision,* their contribution was placed under Power, since they explain the dynamics of power, not decision-making in a community context.

Bachrach and Baratz go further to suggest that one must study "the manner in which the status-quo oriented persons and groups influence those community values and those political institutions . . . which tend to limit the scope of actual decision-making to 'safe' issues." [18] They refer to this as the "restrictive face of power," or the "second face of power." [19]

Status-quo oriented persons also have an institutional advantage in limiting the formal agenda to safe issues. The bias is in the favor of those who wish to restrict rather than those who seek to innovate. As Bachrach and Baratz note:

> While advocates of change must win at all stages of the political process—issue-recognition, decision and implementation of policy —the defenders of existing policy must win at only one stage in the process. It is difficult to avoid the conclusion that all political systems have an inherent 'mobilization of bias' and that this bias strongly favors those currently defending the status quo.[20]

Furthermore, persons advantaged by the existing mobilization of bias will often be willing to make considerable material or economic sacrifices to prevent an alteration of that bias. Persons in positions of power and influence are willing to make considerable concessions to specific grievances, even if the costs are high, to avoid sacrificing or even sharing their privileged position of being able to decide the content of the institutional agenda.[21]

The extent to which institutional agendas are limited to a consideration of safe issues is a matter for further conjecture. Considering the notion that the most important decisions are those that are made to exclude certain items is different from merely studying what happens to an issue when it is on the institutional agenda. Suppression of legitimate grievances to prevent their reaching the formal agenda or the ordering of priorities on an issue spectrum are matters that have only recently been considered.

TYPES OF POWER CONFIGURATIONS AT THE NATIONAL LEVEL. One of the most familiar arguments concerning agenda control at

[18] Bachrach and Baratz, "Two Faces of Power," p. 952.
[19] *Ibid.*, p. 952.
[20] Peter Bachrach and Morton Baratz, *Power and Poverty* (New York: Oxford, 1970), p. 58.
[21] For example, see *Ibid.*, chapters 5–8.

the national level involves a relatively small group of men who allegedly decide what issues are going to be considered. This *power elite,* to use a notion popularized by C. Wright Mills, is dominated by a monolithic military-industrial complex that supposedly controls the most important items on the national agenda through its command over such things as federal grants that permeate the economy. It is further argued that this ruling group will restrict attention to those items that do not threaten its power or interest.[22]

In summary, the indirect ways through which power may be exercised include such phenomena as controlling information and communications, thus restricting what will and will not be considered by decision-makers. Influences upon agenda-building processes, in terms of both what issues are considered and how they are defined, clearly belong in this category. Though they may not always be consciously or explicitly recognized by either the decision-makers or the units exercising them, such forms of control will surely have a marked influence on governmental decisions. To put the matter simply: governmental outputs are in some way a function of the inputs prescribed and proscribed by a formal agenda. This in turn will tend to be a function of prevailing concerns and values that will define what we have called the systemic agenda for political controversy. Thus, in order to understand governmental outputs, consideration of agenda-building processes is imperative. Control of or influence upon those processes must be valued as an important factor in any power equation.[23]

The Decision-Making Approach

Decision-making as an organizing concept is a relatively recent addition to the study of politics. To be sure, contemporary political sci-

[22] C. Wright Mills, *The Power Elite* (New York: Oxford, 1956).
[23] The behavior of both decision-makers and persons attempting to influence decisional processes seem to suggest considerable awareness of such indirect controls. If this is not the case, it would seem that the system has indirect controls that are exercised by persons doing the right things for the wrong reasons—reasons that are perhaps prescribed by the myth or belief system that encompasses the process. The latter is certainly not an unreasonable hypothesis considering we are only now beginning to recognize and explore the role that myths and symbols play in political processes.

ence has profited through case studies emanating from this approach. It has been instrumental in the accumulation and ordering of a considerable body of empirically supported knowledge about legislative, executive, and judicial decisional processes at all governmental levels. Perhaps above all else, the decision-making framework has afforded a refinement of focus that has greatly facilitated political analysis.

COMPONENTS OF DECISION-MAKING ANALYSES. However, for this very reason, it has also tended to restrict our attention to a rather narrow range of political activity.[24] In particular, it has led us to focus primarily on the process of choice *per se*. This focus has meant a concern with the activities and circumstances immediately surrounding and governing the choice of a particular course of action (or inaction) from among a set of alternatives on the basis of some criterion. However, as Herbert Simon has written, "The dynamic theory we are seeking will necessarily be a theory of the whole spectrum of decision-making activity—attention directing, design, and choice—not just a theory of one segment."[25]

INCREMENTALISM AS A FORM OF AGENDA-BUILDING. Another analyst of decisions, Charles Lindblom, has taken a slightly different tack in analyzing how policies are formulated. Lindblom argues that the decision-makers are under pressures of time and incomplete information, and that one of the key foci is the type of strategy devised by the officials to meet the demands of the average day. Lindblom argues that the types of strategies or dodges developed include satisficing (decision-making that aims at acceptable rather than optimal outcomes), refocusing attention on the action taken by the officials, focusing on immediate grievances rather than long range problems, and trying to deal with foreseeable bottlenecks to policies.[26] He as-

[24] It must be noted, however, that some decisional theorists have argued that there is nothing inherent in the decision-making approach that necessarily limits the range of relevant phenomena. Nevertheless, it seems fair to say that in practice the approach has tended to restrict the scope of attention in a fairly severe way.

[25] Herbert Simon, "Political Research: The Decision-Making Framework," a paper delivered at the annual meeting of the American Political Science Association in New York, in September, 1963, p. 5.

[26] For a discussion of the above strategies, see Charles Lindblom, *The Policy-Making Process* (Englewood Cliffs: Prentice-Hall, 1968), pp. 21–27.

serts that many of the classical approaches to the study of decision-making failed to stress the immediate pressures on decision-makers. The "synoptic model of decision-making" fails to take into account the limited problem-solving capabilities of decision-makers, inadequate information, and the costs of analysis.

As a result, what has developed in the American system is a strategy of disjointed incrementalism. This means that only those policies are considered that differ from each other incrementally. Further, only those policies are included that deviate only slightly from the status quo. Examination of a policy means that only marginal differences are emphasized rather than a comprehensive re-examination of a particular policy.

Given these general features of disjointed incrementalism, what types of consequences does it have for the system? First, if those policies that differ slightly from previous ones are considered, then only a small number of issues will ever be on the formal agenda for review. Even among those issues that are considered, only the immediate aspects of the problem are to be reviewed and the decision-makers "often rule out of bounds the uninteresting (to them), the remote, the imponderable, the intangible, and the poorly understood, no matter how important." [27] As a consequence, few alternatives are ever thoroughly examined.

In an evaluation of the American decision to send troops to North Korea, Richard Snyder and Glenn Paige wrote,

> One possible consequence of the single alternative process may be . . . to provide a way of simplifying a situation to the point where action is possible, thus avoiding the complexities of estimate involved in discussing multiple alternatives.[28]

Another feature of incremental decision-making, according to Lindblom, is that objectives are often adjusted to given means in a particular situation. Policy objectives are often developed only when officials inspect what means are available to achieve a particular policy directive. Policies can change not only because one objective be-

[27] David Braybrooke and Charles Lindblom, *A Strategy of Decision* (New York: Free Press, 1963), p. 90.
[28] Richard Snyder and Glenn Paige, "The United States Decision to Resist Aggression in Korea: The Application of an Analytical Scheme," *Administrative Science Quarterly* 3 (1958), p. 376.

comes impossible to achieve, but also because the cost of achieving an objective changes. For example, earlier in the Vietnam war, the American decision-makers thought they had the means to bring a military solution to the conflict. However, as the end dragged on and the body count did not reveal reduced strength on the part of the Vietcong, the decision-makers changed their objective to an "honorable settlement of the war."

A last aspect of incrementalism that touches on agenda-building has to do with serial change. Whenever a particular policy is adopted, it becomes obvious that that issue will be amended slightly as time passes. For example, the Social Security Act has been adjusted constantly since its initial passage. It is assumed that public officials will never "solve" a problem; they will only ameliorate it to some extent each year. Thus, some token step is taken annually to remedy pre-existing problems. This means that the institutional agenda will be clogged with prior problems and that it will be very difficult for a new problem to be placed on the docket or to be given much attention if it does appear.[29]

Decision-making then proceeds according to a process of "mutual adjustment." Given the Lindblom analysis that augurs for a very limited governmental agenda with few new issues being included over time, is there any element of dynamism or innovation within the system? Lindblom argues that there is one factor: multiplicity of decision-makers. In a system such as the American hybrid, there are a great many levels focusing on different problems, and ultimately important social problems may surface on some institutional agenda.[30] Lindblom writes: "They [other decision-makers] will compellingly call to others' attention aspects of the problem they cannot themselves analyze." [31]

[29] For a review of *disjointed incrementalism,* see Braybrooke and Lindblom, *op. cit.,* chapters 3 and 5. A further discussion can be found in Charles Lindblom, *The Intelligence of Democracy* (New York: Free Press, 1965), pp. 137ff; 178ff.

[30] This is similar to the notion of "leverage points," in which there are a number of access points in the decision-making system that are vulnerable to issue penetration. For a review of the concept, see Kenneth Gergen, "Assessing the Leverage Points in the Process of Policy Formation," in Raymond Bauer and Kenneth Gergen (eds.), *The Study of Policy Formation* (New York: Free Press, 1969), 182–83.

[31] Charles Lindblom, *The Intelligence of Democracy,* p. 151.

SUMMARY.   The question of how an issue comes to be on a formal agenda for authoritative decision-making is a crucial aspect of the overall governmental process. An issue must command attention before the choice process begins. Moreover, the way in which an issue is defined when it reaches the attention of decision-makers may well delimit the range of alternatives subsequently considered. In fact, by the time an issue arrives at an actual choice point, its fate may already be decided, for all practical purposes. The crucial questions may be whether or not it gets on the governmental agenda, how it is defined by that time, how visible it is, and what social influences have been activated in the process.

If we are concerned with discovering the rules that govern how particular issues gain access to the agendas of governmental decision-makers, the work of the group theorists should be instructive.

The Group Approach

The importance of groups in the operation of the American polity has been recognized from its inception. The analysis of social processes on the basis of groups has been a major, recurring theme in the study of American politics. The group approach, it is generally agreed, served as one of the major stimuli for the reorientation and development of modern political science (particularly the rediscovery of Arthur Bentley's classic *The Process of Government*). Despite the fact that the approach has suffered considerable criticism—owing largely to the conceptual and operational problems [32] raised by the amorphous nature of groups—the group approach continues to command an important place in the study of politics.

COMPONENTS OF THE GROUP APPROACH.   The perspective suggests that society is fundamentally composed of groups and that social processes must therefore be analyzed as group processes. As David Truman wrote:

> Any society, even one employing the simplest and most primitive techniques, is a mosaic of overlapping groups of various specialized

[32] Cf. Peter Odegard, "A Group Basis of Politics: A New Name for an Ancient Myth," *Western Political Quarterly* 11 (1958), 692–702.

sorts. Through these formations a society is experienced by its members, and in this way it must be observed and understood by its students.[33]

In the process by which policies develop out of a confrontation between a number of groups, how is information transmitted and internalized? Each of the contending parties serves as a filtering device for screening out information that is detrimental to its cause or for reinterpreting that material to provide a different conclusion. The resolution of group conflict would not be so difficult if each group simply attempted to transmit its special interests to the attention of the decision-makers. However, each group reinterprets its interests to be synonymous with the general interest.

Ralph Huitt describes the problem and possible consequences as follows:

> The decision-makers were concerned with promoting the general interest, but so were most of the spokesmen of special interests who appeared before [them]. . . . Social conflict over group interests, clearly perceived and rightly identified, should be easy to mediate; a rough appraisal of the balance of power and frank bargaining should be enough. It is the quantum of concern for the general interest in every calculation that makes the trouble.[34]

In addition, the group perspective must take cognizance of the decision-makers who must attempt to mediate group conflict. Is it possible for them to represent a separate criterion of objectivity, the public interest? After evaluating a Congressional committee, Huitt made the following remarks:

> They [the decision-makers] were not sitting as arbiters of the group struggle, but as participants; it flowed through them. But it was not perceived so clearly and simply as that by those in the struggle. It is generally accepted that there are many opinions, but not that there are many versions of the facts, or at least, not that there is no single true one. This is the crucial problem of communication between groups. . . .[35]

---

[33] David Truman, *The Governmental Process* (New York: Knopf, 1964), p. 43.
[34] Ralph Huitt, "The Congressional Committee: A Case Study," *American Political Science Review* 48 (1954), p. 364.
[35] *Ibid.*

Thus, the decision-makers are caught up in the dialogue between conflicting groups and represent, consciously or unconsciously, the various points at conflict between contending parties.

If group conflicts are taken to be rudimentary social processes, what keeps a society, particularly a democratic one, from being torn apart? Several safeguards are typically cited by group analysts; to wit: groups tend to check one another, giving rise to a sort of dynamic equilibrium; overlapping and multiple group memberships act to mitigate the intensity of group conflicts; and the stability of the system is reinforced by an underlying consensus that puts limits on and provides rules for regulating group conflicts.[36]

THE DEBATE OVER TENETS OF THE "GROUP APPROACH IN AGENDA-BUILDING." A variety of political scientists have adopted the group approach or an offshoot in explaining political phenomena. One of the headings under which analysts are often identified is *pluralism*. In terms of political agenda construction, the main thrust is that politics is a sum total of the struggle between organized groups in an environment in which no one group or set of groups always determines the outcomes over time. As Dahl has written: "It [government] is the steady appeasement of relatively small groups." [37] Dahl describes governmental agenda-building as a fluid process, "one in which there is a high probability that an active and legitimate group in the population can make itself heard effectively at some crucial stage in the process of decision." [38]

Not all analysts accept Dahl's notions of the fluidity of the agenda-building process, since some groups cannot make their demands known to decision-makers and expect some type of responsiveness. Most deprived groups lack the resources of more well-organized groups, so the politics of "access" is limited to those who have the potential for involvement. In addition, decision-makers are likely to

[36] These are only a few of the many that might be mentioned. For a summary discussion of the various institutional and noninstitutional safeguards, see Emmette Redford, "The Never-Ending Search for the Public Interest," in Redford (ed.), *Ideals and Practice in Public Administration* (Montgomery: University of Alabama Press, 1958), pp. 120–35.

[37] Robert Dahl, *A Preface to Democratic Theory* (Chicago: University of Chicago Press, 1956), p. 146.

[38] *Ibid.*, pp. 145–46.

focus on those groups who have supported them in the past. As Michael Lipsky has written:

> When public officials recognize the legitimacy of protest activity, they may not direct public policy toward protest groups at all. Rather, public officials are likely to aim responses at the reference publics from which they originally take their cues.[39]

Others have attacked the universal applicability of group notions. For example, Schattschneider asserts that the approach has been beset with confusions over terminology, and gross exaggerations about the approach can be made. The pressure system, or that sector of politics concerned with pressure group conflict and its resolution, is very small. Schattschneider argues that only certain types of strata are represented in the system and that most people are systematically excluded.

As a consequence, Schattschneider argues that pluralists misconceive the basis of agenda-building. Some conflicts are not resolved in terms of which pressure groups are the largest with the most money. Conflicts are resolved in the public arena beyond the complete control of the interest groups. Most conflicts are not resolved immediately, nor is the outcome a matter of certainty at the outset. Thus, people who view all politics as the interplay of organized groups are missing their dynamic interplay with other relevant mechanisms that come to bear on the problem.[40]

SUMMARY.   Nonetheless, the total group struggle provides a basic source of public issues and prescribes the systemic agenda of controversy. As groups come into conflict with one another, issues are generated that may demand authoritative decisions. A primary function of government, we shall see more clearly, is to manage group conflicts. This is done through the use of legitimacy symbols coupled with authoritative actions of the government. Of course, the question still remains of why some issues come to be on the agendas of gov-

---

[39] Michael Lipsky, "Protest as a Political Resource," *American Political Science Review* 62 (1968), p. 1157.
[40] E. E. Schattschneider, *The Semi-Sovereign People* (New York: Holt, 1960), pp. 20–43. For a more comprehensive critique of pluralism, see William E. Connolly, ed. *The Bias of Pluralism* (New York: Atherton Press, 1969).

ernment while others are excluded. The main answer provided by the group literature is that those groups that are the strongest in some sense will determine what issues are going to be discussed. However, contemporary evidence indicates that that answer is still insufficient to explain the dynamics of agenda-building.

Before pursuing the question of the source of issues receiving agenda attention, let us summarize the types of questions reviewed in an effort to integrate various strains of the literature discussed above.

Clarification of the Problem

We have seen how the problems of agenda-building relate to four leading conceptual orientations for the study of politics. We have found that our concern is essentially with processes occurring at the boundaries of and within the political system. These processes are antecedent to the decision-making sequence in the sense of choice behavior and relate primarily to attention-directing activities. The processes seem to be important not only in determining how problems become issues, or gain standing of the systemic agenda, but also how these issues come to be placed on institutional agendas for authoritative decision-making. The processes also delimit the range of alternatives that will subsequently be designed by the relevant decision-makers. As to the nature of these processes, *group theory* was found suggestive: groups interact and come into conflict, thus giving rise to and defining the systemic agenda, or issues that may provoke an authoritative decisional situation.[41] It was also observed that control over or influence upon the process by which an issue comes to be placed on a governmental agenda is an important source of political power. Given this, we are looking for a clearer understanding of how such power is explained and how and why a group conflict becomes an issue that appears on a formal agenda.

One further point of clarification must be made. We are not

[41] Though it is not at all clear from his discussion, we take this to be an essential part of what Charles Hagan has in mind when he asserts that "values are authoritatively allocated in society through the process of the conflict of groups." This can be found in Charles Hagan, "The Group in Political Science," in Roland Young (ed.), *Approaches to the Study of Politics* (Evanston, Ill.: Northwestern University Press, 1958), p. 40.

asking how groups gain access to decision-makers (though such a query is not necessarily irrelevant to our concerns).[42] We know that groups use multiple means of access to elected leaders. Many of these groups are fairly well identified, and some have been the subject of intensive study.[43] We are asking how issues gain access to an institutional agenda. More specifically, How do group conflicts become transformed into public issues and come to be placed on the docket for authoritative decision-making?

While the generalized schemes discussed earlier identified the answer to that question as essential or at least peripheral to an elaboration of their approaches, our search for an integrated overall conception was not fulfilled. In addition to recognizing that the answer is a crucial aspect of how policies are developed, the discipline must still confront the problems of agenda-building. Thus, we must look elsewhere for other aspects of a scheme that we ultimately hope to develop.

Another area of relevance is *conflict theory,* which has focused on the nature of confrontation between two or more parties and how systemic and institutional agendas are determined by the type of competition between sides. The next chapter will review features of the conflict approach that have relevance for the problem of issue creation and formal agenda access. While we cannot hope for conclusive answers, we can outline some aspects of the process through which issues are transformed into problems confronting policy-makers.

[42] This relates more to the direct exercise of power discussed above. It seems to be the sort of thing Truman is primarily concerned with when he uses the term "access." See Truman, *op. cit.,* pp. 321–51.

[43] For example, see Redford, *op. cit.,* pp. 118–19.

3

Approaches to the Study of Conflict Management

The functions of government have been described and classified in many ways. However, most of the manifest social functions may be conveniently subsumed under two broad categories: service and conflict management.[1] The service functions refer roughly to authoritative decision-making related to essentially uncontested, generally agreed upon, or consensual demands. The conflict management function, on the other hand, relates to the authoritative treatment of issues, or contested demands. It is that function upon which we will focus.

According to Banfield and Wilson, the management of social conflict is the distinctly "political" function of government.[2] Though it is doubtful that much can be gained through trying to define "political," we would have to agree that social conflict and its management are necessary ingredients in any conception of politics. As Easton has observed: "conflicts over demands constitute the flesh and blood of all political systems, from the smallest to the largest and from the simplest to the most complex." [3]

[1] Edward Banfield and James Wilson, *City Politics* (Cambridge: Harvard University Press, 1965), pp. 18–19.
[2] *Ibid.*
[3] David Easton, *A Systems Analysis of Political Life* (New York: Wiley, 1965), p. 48.

Political systems without conflict have existed only in the minds of Utopian thinkers.[4] The fact that most positive Utopias from Plato's *Republic* to Skinner's *Walden Two* can be characterized by the absence of social conflict seems, itself, to be an indication of the prominence and pervasiveness of conflict in the "normal" operations of a society. One of the primary distinctions between Utopian and more "realistic" conceptions of social processes has to hinge on the way in which conflict is treated.[5]

It will, therefore, be assumed that "conflict between groups is a fundamental social process," [6] and that the management of such conflict is a primary way in which "government functions to establish and maintain a measure of order in the relationship among groups. . . ." [7]

To avoid a possible source of confusion about what is and what is not meant by the conflict management function of government, it must be noted that the term does not imply that governmental decision-makers are necessarily detached from social conflict and sit as judges or referees while extra-governmental groups compete. Seldom, if ever, will we find the men of government sitting as a disinterested third party that simply "ratifies the victories of successful coalitions, and records the terms of the surrenders, compromises and conquests. . . ." [8] Quite to the contrary, we may expect governmental decision-makers frequently to be full participants in group conflicts.[9] However, their participation in no way denies their conflict management role. That role accrues from the simple fact that their decisions are in some way binding.

[4] Herbert Spiro has argued that "while the basic prerequisite for community is *consensus,* though minimally only on common goals. . . , the basic prerequisite for a political system is *dissensus.* Politics arises out of disagreement . . ." We concur. See Herbert Spiro, "Comparative Politics: A Comprehensive Approach," *American Political Science Review* 56 (1962), p. 577.

[5] For an excellent discussion and analysis of Utopian formulations, see Theodore Caplow, *Principles of Organization* (New York: Harcourt, 1964), pp. 291–316.

[6] Robert Dubin, "Industrial Conflict and Social Welfare," *Journal of Conflict Resolution* 1 (1957), p. 183.

[7] David Truman, *The Governmental Process* (New York: Knopf, 1951), p. 45.

[8] Earl Latham, "The Group Basis of Politics: Notes for a Theory," *American Political Science Review* 46 (1952), p. 390.

[9] For example, see Ralph Huitt, "The Congressional Committee: A Case Study," *American Political Science Review* 48 (1954), pp. 340–65; or James Rosenau, *Public Opinion and Foreign Policy* (New York: Random House, 1961), passim.

This chapter first describes the conflict perspective from a static stance, then describes the sources of conflict. It then considers conflict as a dynamic process and reviews two approaches having portent for agenda-making. It also evaluates other elements, such as the objectives of competing parties, violence, and the frequency of conflict. Finally, it considers the language of the disputants as a critical element in determining the likelihood of an issue attaining access to a political agenda. At that point the literature on symbols and their uses in politics is briefly reviewed.

Conflict: Static Description

Given conflict management as a basic function of government, we may ask why and how certain conflicts become issues that require governmental action. To answer these questions, we must consider the nature of social conflict itself.

Despite the existence of a large literature dealing with conflict, the concept remains broad and ill-defined. Consistent with much of the current literature, we will beg the question of offering a precise definition of the concept and will simply attempt to describe relevant characteristics. For the present, our discussion will be confined to a more or less static description, though later, we will attempt to focus more closely on the dynamics of social conflict.

Social conflict refers to a particular type of interaction between two or more units. We wish to characterize that interaction. First, however, a few preliminary remarks are in order.

PRESENT CONTEXT. Although social conflict can and does occur at a number of different levels (that is, between units varying from individuals to nation-states or even larger units), our concern is only with conflict as it occurs within the American social system—domestic conflict of essentially a non-violent nature occurring within the context of the explicit and implicit rules defined by our culture and social structure. Further, we are primarily concerned with group as opposed to individual conflict and mediated as opposed to face-to-face conflict.[10]

---

[10] *Group* is used in a generic sense to refer to any plurality of individuals banding together formally or informally, temporarily or relatively permanently to promote or protest a shared perception of mutual interest (Cf. David Truman, *op. cit.*, p. 33). We are restricting ourselves to mediated conflict because there is some evidence to suggest that the role of government vis-a-vis face-

ALTERNATIVE CONCEPTUAL PERSPECTIVES.   In conceptualizing conflict, at least two alternatives are available. First, we may speak of internal, or intra-unit, conflict. Perhaps the best example of this is the psychological model of conflict, wherein the dispute occurs within the individual.[11] However, as Parsons, Deutsch, and others have shown, it is possible to view a collectivity as a similar system; that is, multiple-person behavior units may at times be appropriately regarded as " 'epi-organisms' possessing as systems many of the system properties of organisms." [12]

The second perspective from which conflict may be viewed is that of inter-system, or inter-unit, interaction (i.e., external conflict). Viewed in this way, conflict is characterized by two or more competing parties, each attempting to control the allocation or distribution of some valued, scarce thing or things.[13]

A given conflict may be conceived as either external or internal. The perspective used is dependent upon the level and units of analysis used, as well as the questions being asked. Here we will have occasion to use both conceptions. While the bulk of the analysis will be based on the external perspective, it will be useful, particularly in attempting to characterize the dynamics of conflict, to consider the conflictual situation as a system and to employ the internal perspective. An effort will be made throughout to make clear which conception is being employed.

Conditions and Sources of Social Conflict

The fundamental condition of social conflict is scarcity.[14] As Easton has pointed out, "the fundamental fact confronting all societies is

to-face conflict tends to differ from that with respect to mediated conflict. For example, see Arthur Vidich and Joseph Bensman, *Small Town and Mass Society* (Garden City: Doubleday & Company, 1960).

[11] Cf. Judson Brown, "Principles of Intrapersonal Conflict," *Journal of Conflict Resolution,* 1 (1957), pp. 135–54.

[12] Kenneth Boulding, "Organization and Conflict," *Journal of Conflict Resolution,* 1 (1957), p. 129.

[13] Cf. Raymond Mack and Richard Snyder, "The Analysis of Social Conflict —Toward an Overview and Synthesis," *Journal of Conflict Resolution* 1 (1957), pp. 211–48. For a more recent review of conceptual approaches to the study of conflict, see Clinton Fink, "Some Conceptual Difficulties in the Theory of Social Conflict," *Journal of Conflict Resolution* 12 (1968), pp. 412–60.

[14] Mack and Snyder, *op. cit.,* p. 218. Also see William Mitchell, *The American Polity* (New York: Free Press, 1962), p. 275.

that scarcity of some valued things prevails. It leads to disputes over their allocation." [15] The meaning of scarcity is, of course, highly relative, varying with time and place. The relevant scarcity need not be "in any absolute sense but in light of the expectations of the members of society." [16]

The types of scarcity that may serve as the referent objects of conflict are manifold.[17] They include not only tangible or material resources (or symbols of such) but also positions (such as those of power, prestige, and respect). Furthermore, social conflicts may be ideational or symbolic as well as instrumental.[18] The objects of conflict need not be specific but can be highly abstract.

In assuming that there are two basic categories of objects of conflict (viz., scarce *positions* and scarce *resources*),[19] we are not suggesting that all conflicts necessarily refer to substantive allocations, even in the abstract. Clearly, conflicts vis-a-vis a given object may be procedural as well as substantive (that is, conflicts may arise not only over *who gets what* but also over *how*).[20]

Even with this qualification, it may be objected that we are being too restrictive, that we are allowing for only "realistic" con-

[15] David Easton, *A Framework for Political Analysis* (Englewood Cliffs: Prentice-Hall, 1965), p. 53.

[16] *Ibid.,* p. 80.

[17] Though a bit tangential to our main purpose, we might digress briefly to speculate about how one might categorize those scarce things that serve as objects of conflict. Noting that by definition these scarce things are valued, we might take the list of values posited by Harold Lasswell as a starting point for the development of a typology of potential sources of social conflict. Although Lasswell's list refers to individual values, it seems reasonable to assume that individual values are largely fulfilled through group processes. Consequently, such a list might provide a convenient place to begin. An alternative strategy might be to start with the hierarchical system of basic needs set forth by Maslow. Yet another alternative might be found in the work of Eric Erikson. Though we shall not pursue the task here, such an effort seemingly would be quite worthwhile. As here conceived, the problem would appear to complement the work of Christian Bay, *The Structure of Freedom* (New York: Atheneum Publishers, 1965); and James Davies, *Human Nature in Politics* (New York: Wiley, 1963).

[18] Mack and Snyder, *op. cit.,* p. 216. Also see Murray Edelman, *The Symbolic Uses of Politics* (Urbana: University of Illinois Press, 1964).

[19] This distinction is that made by Mack and Snyder, *op. cit.,* but it also corresponds roughly with the two major kinds of issues distinguished by David Easton (viz., decisional and orientational). See *Systems Analysis of Political Life,* p. 142.

[20] Cf. Herbert Spiro, *op. cit.,* p. 577.

flicts.[21] If we limit ourselves strictly to conflicts arising from the incompatibility of the needs and wants of two or more groups owing to scarcity, what about "nonrealistic" conflicts, wherein the source is not scarcity but internal tension or frustration? [22] Presumably, the conflicting interests in realistic conflicts can in some way be reconciled, but nonrealistic conflict may persist with no allocative or distributive outcome satisfying the disputants.

The position taken here is that whether a conflict is realistic or nonrealistic, it will at any point in time have some scarce thing as a referent. This allows us to avoid the perplexing problems of trying to distinguish one type from the other.[23]

Multi-party Conflicts and the Effect of Time

In a multi-party conflict situation, the protagonists may immediately arrive at some collective reconciliation, thus moving the situation to one of trading or accommodation; or one or more of the parties may simply opt out of the conflict. If, however, the situation remains conflictual, it is almost axiomatic that the remaining parties will align themselves into two camps (that is, multi-conflicts will tend to become two-party conflicts).[24]

If the parties remain in conflict over a sustained period of time, the conflict will tend to become institutionalized, and accommodation will be routinized.[25] Participants will agree on the issues involved

[21] Lewis Coser, *The Functions of Social Conflict* (New York: Free Press, 1956), pp. 48–55.

[22] *Ibid.*

[23] At least on the level of overt behavior, it is not at all clear how one could distinguish between realistic and nonrealistic conflict. The fact that a sequence of conflicts is generated, one immediately after another, surely does not imply that the disputes are nonrealistic, even if the same parties are involved throughout. Moreover, even if the sequence arises from a nonrealistic source, it seems likely that the series will, on the manifest level, involve a number of discrete conflicts, each defined differently and with differing objects of response. As Edelman, *op. cit.*, has observed, success, even in realistic conflicts, most often leads to new demands and not retirement from the field (pp. 152–71); therefore, who can say a given sequence of conflicts is nonrealistic? Since there seems to be no reason to assume, at least in the context of the American political system, that the character, logic, or dynamics of these two types of conflict are fundamentally different, we will make no such distinction.

[24] Mack and Snyder, *op. cit.*, p. 321.

[25] Dubin, *op. cit.*, p. 187.

and their specific definition. More than likely, they will also agree on the general procedures for resolving differences.[26] Such conflicts tend to remain "private," or limited in scope.

The Dynamics of Social Conflict

Until now conflict has been viewed as essentially static (that is, well-defined, with given characteristics along various dimensions). However, social conflict is not static, but rather highly fluid and elastic. Moreover, despite the diversity of sources and precipitating events, social conflicts, once they have begun, "resemble each other remarkably." [27] As James Coleman notes: "It is the peculiarity of social controversy that it sets in motion its own dynamics; these tend to carry it forward in a path which bears little relation to its beginnings." [28] Given the general characteristics of conflict outlined above, an attempt can now be made to outline its dynamics.

Schattschneider has observed: "At the nub of politics are, first, the way in which the public participates in the spread of conflict, and second, the processes by which the unstable relation of the public to the conflict is controlled." [29] Of concern, then, is the scope of a conflict's contagion and the determinants of that scope.

Given this general background in the conflict perspective, What types of insights exist in the literature that might illuminate the agenda-building process? Gamson asserts that there have been two approaches to the study of conflict. The first stresses group phenomena, with organized collectivities fighting over the allocation of resources. The second refers to social control, emphasizing the potentialities of the system to control the development of controversy.[30]

Both perspectives are useful in understanding the genesis of political agendas. The first provides a means of analyzing conflicts in terms of group splits and alerts us to key cleavage lines that may determine how issues appear on a formal agenda; the second stresses an

---

[26] An example of this type of situation would be labor-management conflicts.

[27] James Coleman, *Community Conflict* (Glencoe: Free Press, 1957), p. 9.

[28] *Ibid.*, pp. 9–10.

[29] E. E. Schattschneider, *The Semi-Sovereign People* (New York: Holt, 1960), p. 3.

[30] William Gamson, *Power and Discontent* (Homewood, Ill.: Dorsey Press, 1968), Chapter 1.

awareness of the system properties leading to conflict regulation. Conflict is a dynamic process with reciprocal relations between competing parties within a system and the system's political decision-makers. This interaction is crucial to the determination of which issues will be considered and which will be excluded from consideration.

THE THREE CRUCIAL DIMENSIONS OF A CONFLICT SITUATION. Before reviewing specific approaches to the study of conflict in an agenda-building context, let us delineate three standard dimensions of any conflict situation involving two or more parties. These elements include scope, intensity, and visibility. The first two relate to the actual conflict itself, viewed as a system; the last, to the conflict in the context of the larger social milieu.[31]

Scope refers to the extensity of a conflict—the number of persons and groups who have actually aligned themselves in a conflict. At any point in time, scope will include those persons or groups who were initially involved, plus any persons or groups who have subsequently been drawn into the controversy. Clearly, the scope of a conflict will depend on the number of persons who value the scarce things at issue. More immediately, it will be a function of the organizational scale of the parties in conflict.

The *intensity* of a conflict relates to the degree of commitment of the contending parties to mutually incompatible positions. It will be directly linked to the "dearness," or value saliency, attached to the objects of conflict by those involved. Operationally, intensity will roughly correspond to the resources the contending parties are willing to commit to the conflict relative to their total capability. All conflicts have a cost dimension, and the more vital the objects of a conflict are to a group (or are perceived to be), the more of the group's resources it will be willing to commit to the conflict. Intensity, then, is a function of both the degree of commitment of the contending parties and the degree to which their respective commitments are mutually incompatible.

Visibility is the variable linking a conflict with its publics. It indicates the number of persons or groups that will be aware of a conflict and its possible consequences. The visibility of a conflict will

[31] Schattschneider, *op. cit.*, passim.

be a function of both its scope and intensity, as well as its definition. Visibility is a critical variable in that it is necessary for the expansion of a conflict, which in turn will bear on the probable access of an issue to a governmental agenda.

THE STUDY OF ISSUE CONFLICT. One of the first analysts to apply notions of social conflict to the study of public issue formation was E. E. Schattschneider. In an initial conflict situation, he argues, there are two primary ingredients: the size or the number of people committed to each issue position; and the intensity of commitment, or how strongly the members of the competing groups feel about their proposal or the stance of the other group. The initial composition of strength is only a beginning point, however. As Schattschneider points out, the party that has the greatest number of adherents with the most intense commitment at the inception has no guarantee that its issue stance will have sway or will receive the attention of authoritative decision-makers.[32]

If the initial disposition of a conflict were the determinant, most issues would never gain standing on a political agenda, since the side with the widest and most intense support would always succeed. However, to get an issue on the docket, one side or the other must enlist more support for its position by changing the cleavage lines or substituting one conflict for another. Schattschneider uses the term *redefinition* to describe this process. The redefinition phase is critical in determining whether or not a particular issue will receive formal agenda attention.

The redefinition process is illustrated by the recent fluoridation disputes. In general, the initial controversy dealt with adding minute quantities of fluoride to the water supply to reduce tooth decay. In several communities, however, this issue was redefined by antagonists to be, not a health issue (although the question of whether or not fluoride was poisonous was raised), but rather a matter involving the violation of individual rights and the intrusion of government into private realms.[33]

The gun control controversy illustrates attempts both to enlarge and to limit (or privatize) the scope of a conflict. The issue initially

[32] Schattschneider, *op. cit.*, pp. 1–19, 47–77.
[33] William Gamson, "The Fluoridation Dialogue," *Public Opinion Quarterly* 25 (1961), pp. 526–37.

centered on whether or not more restrictive gun legislation would reduce the incidence of homicide and other violent crimes. The issue was quickly redefined by both sides. The supporters of gun control legislation argued that such legislation would be almost a sure cure to many of the major problems of crime control, overlooking the easily availability of illegal weapons to those bent on crime. Rather than focusing on whether or not the control of firearms would mean fewer violent deaths, opponents of such legislation concentrated on what owning a gun meant to certain people (for example, sportsmen) and insisted that the Constitution guaranteed the right to "keep and bear arms," neglecting to mention that the courts have not upheld this interpretation of the Second Amendment. In the words of an executive official of the National Rifle Association: "The man with the gun, the citizen properly trained in the use of firearms, has been the foundation of . . . our nation." [34]

An example of redefinition through the simplification of an issue is provided by the response of the American Medical Association to Medicare and other health programs. The AMA has been quick to identify such government-sponsored programs with socialized medicine and has issued statements like: "If the doctors lose their freedom today—if their patients are regimented tomorrow, who will be next? YOU WILL BE NEXT." [35]

Perhaps the most effective way to restrict or localize the scope of an issue is to redefine it technically so that most people will not understand it. For example, Congressional passage of the Taft-Hartley bill was greatly facilitated by its having been defined as essentially a technical matter. As a consequence, it did not arouse widespread union hostility. [36]

Related to the process of redefinition is the phenomenon of displacement. At times an issue may develop that seemingly has the potential to gain formal agenda access, but it is sidetracked by the sudden development of another issue that repolarizes existing cleavage lines. For example, in Philadelphia, the issue of school bussing was displaced by the issue of crime in schools and pupil safety.

The potential number of people who can be mobilized in any

[34] Richard Harwood, "The Public Besieges the Gun Lobby," *Washington Post,* June 23, 1968, p. 35.
[35] Truman, *op. cit.,* p. 231.
[36] *Ibid.,* pp. 194–95.

conflict is limited. Using nonvoting as a criterion, Schattschneider suggests that because they have limited information and interest, about 40 percent of the adult population are not appealed to by groups seeking to promote an issue to agenda status. Even then, he argues, when groups appeal for support, they do not beseech the remaining 60 percent that is potentially mobilizable, but appeal only to relevant subgroups within the populace. The limited pool of mobilizable human resources is an important ingredient in the recipe of issue expansion. If an issue can be expanded to include previously uninvolved people, access to a formal agenda may be achieved even though the numbers are not overwhelming.[37]

Using a scheme that closely resembles that of Schattschneider, James Coleman has explored how issues gain agenda access in the context of local level politics.[38] However, his model of community controversy applies to all levels of government. He approaches the study of issue conflict in terms of an initial controversy between two groups with a largely disinterested and apathetic public. The public is brought into the conflict primarily through a series of errors committed by the leaders of the community that activates the passive mass or causes a change in popular opinion. When this occurs, the group benefitting from the changed mood of the public utilizes the popular response to put its claim on the public docket. For example, a group opposing a certain book in the local library because it is "obscene" might contend that it is part of a "communist conspiracy" to put such books in libraries throughout the nation to corrupt young minds. Such an argument might arouse fear and suspicion in the community and lead to an opinion change concerning library policies.

Coleman argues that vituperative conflicts tend to be the ones that gain the most ready access to the governmental agenda. He asserts that there is a Gresham's Law concerning issues, in that vitriolic disputes that portend disruption tend to command attention while conflicts over substantive issues without much accompanying animosity tend to be pushed aside. He notes, however, that there are certain strategies that can be used to contain vitriolic issues and preclude them from attaining formal governmental consideration.

---

[37] *Ibid.*
[38] Coleman, *op. cit.*, passim.

One means of controlling conflict expansion is through cooptation. For example, a leader of a group with a grievance is brought into the structure (i.e., the government) and given a title and perfunctory duties. Similarly, appointing a group official to the bureaucracy may create the impression that the group's grievance is being considered, when in fact, the tactic is used as a means to avoid having to come to grips with the problem. Cooptation has been a fairly common practice with respect to civil rights. Typically, a beleaguered public official either appoints a black or rigs an election so that a black can win office and then draws attention to the success and accomplishments of this black man rather than placing the minority group grievances on the formal agenda.

Other factors that may preclude a specific grievance from commanding formal attention include variation in community identification and the type of voluntary group structure that exists within the local community. Coleman suggests that severe conflicts may be avoided if most citizens have a strong identification with the local community. By exploiting this sense of identification, established interests may prevent a grievance from being heard, arguing that for the good of the community, it is better not to risk disruption of the prevailing "harmony."

According to Coleman, organizational or group memberships affect conflict in two ways. First, multiple group memberships cross-pressure the individual and thus tend to mediate the intensity of conflict. As a member of the Democratic Party, an individual may endorse the idea of equal treatment of all minority groups; but as a member of a local union, he may resist black intrusions into his work group because of the threat it poses to his job. Second, the greater the proportion of the community that is involved in various types of groups, the greater the number of people who are potentially mobilizable, and thus the greater the likelihood that issue redefinition can bring a larger number into the fray.[39]

EMPIRICAL STUDIES OF CONFLICT AT THE COMMUNITY LEVEL. After studying how fluoridation decisions were made in ten Massachusetts cities, Irwin Sanders concluded that conflicts go through

---

[39] For a general review of Coleman's conflict approach and the means by which conflict can be controlled, see Coleman, *op. cit.*, pp. 7–22.

certain identifiable phases in reaching the formal agenda. At the initiation phase, the conflict is confined to the initial disputants, in this case to medical officials who believe that fluoridating the water supplies may have certain benefits. Additional phases include searching for additional support, presenting the program to supporters, and discussing what type of action should be taken. The focus is then shifted to pressuring local decision-makers to put the issue on the agenda. If the leaders accede and select an option, the opponents of the program may attempt to put the issue back on the agenda to reformulate it or defeat it. In such a situation, the process becomes continuous, since the issue goes through a series of redefinitions.[40]

In a more elaborate study of fluoridation cases, Robert Crain and his associates tried to ascertain how fluoridation controversies develop and the type of attention they receive from local authorities. The authors found that the more vitriolic the dispute between fluoridation supporters and detractors, the greater the likelihood that the local decision-makers would take the matter under advisement. A frequent response was to put the matter to popular vote, where it often met defeat. Even when it passed, such opposition was often generated in the community during the course of the campaign that decision-makers were reluctant to take any assertive action for fear of arousing further controversy.

In most instances, the authors found that if the item was placed on an institutional agenda, the opponents were able to defeat the program simply because they could inculcate enough fear and uncertainty in the citizens to lead to a negative response. One of the problems of getting the fluoridation issue on an institutional agenda arose from the misplaced enthusiasm of its supporters, who acted too hastily, thereby generating unnecessary emotional opposition.

The fluoridation controversies tended to resemble what Coleman called disruptive issue conflicts, in that the issues were highly charged with emotion, with each side being strongly critical of its opponent. The opponents of fluoridation were more likely to use unethical tactics, while supporters felt more bound by some sense of ethical conduct. This situation tended to work to the benefit of the detractors, who were able to enlarge public support for their position

---

[40] Irwin Sanders, "The Stages of a Community Controversy: The Case of Fluoridation," *Journal of Social Issues* 17 (1961), pp. 55–65.

by spreading wild, false stories about the potential impact of fluoridation.[41]

Another attempt to examine some of Coleman's contentions in a community setting was undertaken by William Gamson, who examined a number of local conflicts in several New England towns. He differentiated between two types of conflict: conventional splits, in which each party believes that the other side used legitimate means to achieve its ends, regardless of the outcome; and rancorous conflicts, in which one or both sides thinks the other used unfair tactics or unscrupulous methods to achieve its objectives.

To a student of agenda-building, such a distinction might be crucial, because when parties use unorthodox methods to advance their cause, they may have a greater chance of forcing the decision-makers to consider their position. After considering a wide range of issues such as fluoridation, Gamson found shifts in political control of the community to be particularly useful in predicting the likelihood of rancorous conflicts. When the ethnic composition of an area was changing, particularly in terms of who controlled key offices, there was a greater likelihood that one ethnic group would see the other as resorting to underhanded methods to achieve its objectives.[42]

In reviewing his findings, Gamson stresses the role of language in the development of issue conflicts. He writes: "In the issues studied here, it is frequently . . . the case that the targets of rancor be regarded as agents or dupes of intricate conspiracies aimed at removing precious freedom, or as tools of a giant power grab." [43] This relates to Coleman's contention that redefinition of a conflict to move it from a specific context to a more general level is an important ingredient in making the issue more palatable to larger segments of the community.[44]

Another attempt to subject some of Coleman's contentions to empirical analysis was undertaken by Herbert Danzger, who investigated civil rights issues in seventeen Southern communities. Danzger

[41] Robert Crain, Elihu Katz, and Donald Rosenthal, *The Politics of Community Conflict: The Fluoridation Decision* (Indianapolis: Bobbs-Merrill Company, 1969). The chapters most relevant to the study of agenda-building are 1, 4, 6, 8, and 11.
[42] William Gamson, "Rancorous Conflict in Community Politics," *American Sociological Review* 31 (1966), pp. 71–81.
[43] *Ibid.*, p. 80.
[44] Coleman, *op. cit.*, p. 10.

was interested in such variables as duration of the conflict, legitimacy of the tactics used, extent of violence, and type of outcome. The parties in conflict were categorized by their numerical strength, the type of group structure, and the background of supporters.

Danzger also differentiates between vertical and horizontal organization. Horizontal organization refers to associations within the community, while vertical ties refer to linkages to groupings outside the community. Danzger found that integrationists initiated most of the conflicts and most frequently attempted to place the race issue on the formal agenda of the local community. He also found that outside groups were quite active in pushing the integrationists' arguments in public issue debates. "Actors outside the community raised issues three times as often for the integrationists." [45] This finding tends to indicate that organizations outside of the community in which the battle is being fought are quite instrumental in the inception of conflict, as well as in its expansion.

In addition, Danzger found that the type of groups involved in issue conflict differed once the issue was expanded beyond the local community. Integrationists relied to a greater extent on nationwide groupings to back their cause than did the segregationists, who relied primarily on local groupings. As Danzger notes, "Such [nationwide] support may be necessary if there is to be an attempt to introduce substantial change in a community regarding a specific issue." [46] In agenda terms, the type of issue itself will be a determinant of the likelihood that a group will seek aid outside the community.

A SUMMARY OF THE DYNAMICS OF CONFLICT EXPANSION. According to Schattschneider and Coleman, there are several mechanisms through which the scope of a conflict may be expanded. Some of these may become operative through the intentional action of the contending parties; others, however, are in a sense involuntarily activated and arise from certain social-psychological facts. Because of the latter in particular, "the scope of a conflict can be most easily restricted at the very beginning." [47]

---

[45] Herbert Danzger, "A Quantified Description of Community Conflict," *American Behavioral Scientist* 12, No. 2 (1968), p. 11.

[46] *Ibid.*, p. 12. For a review of the findings, see *Ibid.*, pp. 9–14.

[47] Schattschneider, *op. cit.*, p. 4.

Whether or not the scope of a conflict will be expanded will depend in large measure upon the definition of the issues involved. If the original disputants can agree upon a definition of the issues using the various dimensions discussed above, it is likely that the conflict will remain restricted and largely private to the original parties.[48] In such a case the outcome of the conflict will be primarily a function of the relative strengths of the contestants.

However, if the contending parties cannot agree on the issues, it is likely that the conflict will be communicated to others. Parties may fail to agree upon a definition of issues when: (1) one or more of the parties finds itself particularly disadvantaged by a particular definition and the consequences are unacceptable; (2) one or more of the parties has potential strength outside the specific conflict that can be aroused to the advantage of that party; or (3) there are fundamentally different perceptions of what the conflict involves. While the immediate result of defining a conflict more broadly may be to the advantage of one of the parties, the cycle does not necessarily end there. It may be repeated time after time, every change having its bias. Once the process has been set in motion and more people become involved, "the original participants are apt to lose control of the conflict altogether." [49]

As the scope of a conflict expands, so does its visibility, thus contributing to its further expansion and also to the probability of its governmental management. This process is facilitated by the fact that the "issues which provide the initial basis of response in a controversy undergo great transformation." [50]

Generally speaking, the issues tend to become more abstract and ambiguous as a conflict is expanded.[51] Specific issues give way to more general ones, complex issues are simplified and distorted,[52] and new and different issues are generated.[53]

[48] For example, see *Ibid.*, p. 3.
[49] Schattschneider, *loc. cit.*
[50] Coleman, *op. cit.*, p. 10.
[51] Cf. Edelman, *op. cit.*, pp. 114–94.
[52] "It is characteristic of larger numbers of people in our society that they see and think in terms of stereotypes, personalization, and over-simplifications, that they cannot recognize or tolerate ambiguous situations, and that they accordingly respond chiefly to symbols that over-simplify and distort." *Ibid.*, p. 31.
[53] According to Coleman, *op. cit.*, p. 10, "[t]here are two different sources for

Though the blurring of issues seemingly would suggest that the intensity of a conflict would be attenuated, that is not necessarily the case. "People read their own meanings into situations that are unclear or provocative of emotion." [54] The expanding scope of a conflict is likely to cause various symbols and values to be conjured up, posing a threat to popular beliefs and values. Also, the increasing scope of a conflict tends to polarize social relations, which in turn reinforces the cleavage and tends to increase the intensity of hostility.[55]

As we have previously observed, the expanding scope and increasing intensity of a conflict tend to increase its visibility, thus making it more likely that it will become an issue on some governmental agenda.[56] The level of government at which an issue enters is also a function of these variables. Generally, the greater the scope, intensity, and visibility of a conflict, the higher the level of government at which an issue will enter.[57]

So far we have focused on how a conflict may expand or intensify. Both the Schattschneider and the Coleman approaches assume that the conflict will necessarily expand. Are there any ways to curb this process? Certainly, it would seem that the groups in a conflict would attempt to control those factors that affect its outcome. While this is true, once the expansion of a conflict begins, it is far more difficult to control it than to expand the dispute.

---

this diversification of issues. One is in a sense 'involuntary'; issues which could not have been raised before the controversy spring suddenly to the fore as the relationships between groups and individuals change. . . . As long as functioning relations exist between individuals or groups, there are strong inhibitions upon introducing any issue which might impair the functioning. . . . But in many other cases, illustrated by political disputes, the diversification of issues is a more purposive move . . . to solidify opinion and bring new participants by providing new bases of response."

[54] Edelman, *op. cit.,* p. 30.

[55] This occurs because of the psychological processes of consistency and generalization. Men have a strong need for consistency and thus tend to see all acts by an opponent from whom they are isolated as hostile. This is exacerbated by reinforcement from their own side.

[56] The mass media serves as an important vehicle for increasing the visibility of a conflict. Politicians, too, both aspirant and incumbent, may serve as an important tool, actually coopting an issue.

[57] Jack Peltason, *Federal Courts in the Political Process* (Garden City: Doubleday, 1955), p. 19.

Other Salient Elements in the Study of Conflict

CONFLICT TERMINATION.   Lewis Coser argues that one of the most important features of any conflict between two or more parties is what the parties agree to consider a termination of the conflict. He notes:

> Once a goal has been reached by one of the parties and this is accepted as a clue to the acceptance of defeat by the other, the conflict is ended. The more restricted the object of contention and the more visible for both parties the clues to victory, the higher the chances that the conflict will be limited in time and extension.[58]

For example, a dispute between labor and management may be more easily resolved by the parties concerned, and not become a concern for government, when each side responds to cues given by the other as to methods for resolving the conflict. When conflicts are multi-faceted, the parties involved have greater difficulty in working out a solution, and the pressure for formal agenda access becomes greater.[59]

NATURE OF ISSUE CONFLICT.   The frequency of issue conflicts and the nature of the cleavage will also affect the type of termination. For example, Theodore Caplow asserts that most patterns of conflict fall into three different categories: episodic, continuous, and terminal.[60] Since terminal conflict involves the annihilation of the opponent, it is of little relevance to the present inquiry. Thus, we will consider only the first two categories.

In an episodic conflict, the split between groups will last over an extended period of time. Both sides recognize the rewards involved, and each realizes that the conflict will reoccur at certain fairly regular intervals. Most collective bargaining encounters are of this type. Since certain types of conflicts will spill over into the public realm if not settled (e.g., steel, automobile, and railroad industries), the resul-

[58] Lewis Coser, *Continuities in the Study of Social Conflict* (New York: Free Press, 1967), p. 43.

[59] For a more thorough review of conflict termination, see *Ibid.*, pp. 39–51.

[60] Theodore Caplow, *Principles of Organization* (New York: Harcourt, 1964), pp. 326–65.

tant issues have an almost built-in access to the governmental agenda if a solution is not found quickly by the original disputants.

Another type of episodic conflict relates to what might be called the "long, hot summer mentality." Around June, decision-makers collectively brace themselves for a series of violent outbursts in the ghettos and provide token concessions to prevent an insurrection or an accelerated level of violence. As the summer ends, minority group demands lose their high priority and indeed may disappear from the docket until the following June.

In the case of continuous conflict, the strategies of competing parties become more complex, with both sides being aware that even momentary resolution of the dispute may take some time. For example, supporters of planned parenthood had to work for a number of years before decision-makers even considered birth control to be an issue warranting governmental attention. Caplow cites perceptual distortion as one of the characteristics of this form of conflict. Stereotyping opponents plays an important role. As he writes, "Its mildest form is the assumption, almost unavoidable . . . that all members of the enemy think and respond alike. Personification is often more literal than this and the enemy organization is visualized as an evil giant." [61] Thus, how groups tend to perceive each other and how that perception relates to public behavior may be important determinants of whether that issue will gain the recognition of decision-makers.

ROLE OF VIOLENCE. Another consideration in the study of agenda-building concerns the utilization of violence as a means of achieving some degree of recognition by decision-makers.[62] When an organized group has been prevented from attaining tangible benefits from the system for a long time, it may be ready to use extralegal means to achieve a place on the governmental agenda. H. L. Nieburg has written that all social systems are dynamic and in a state of flux. One way for groups "outside" the political system (i.e., those denied access in the past) to gain admission is through committing a series

[61] Caplow, *op. cit.*, p. 353.

[62] Gamson identifies violence as one of the ways in which systems can be transformed in terms of the types of groups that are going to have access. Others he lists are (1) crisis, such as a depression or a defeat in a foreign war; (2) governmental activity that exacerbates the initial cleavage; and (3) activities by pressure groups that were formed initially for non-political ends. See Gamson, "Stable Unrepresentation in American Society," pp. 20–21.

of violent acts, such as rioting. Extended violence will not be required, according to Nieburg, since decision-makers will soon realize that it is much easier to place the grievances of the group on the formal agenda than to suppress the group.

Nieburg contends that the principal purpose of overt violence is to establish the credibility of the group in the eyes of the decision-makers. Once that has been achieved, the group should be able to rely on the threat to commit further violence without actually committing disruptive acts. In fact, threats of violence rather than acts of violence are one of the most common means by which new or deprived groups gain entry into the legitimate political arena. If the group loses its credibility, however, a series of violent acts may be required to demonstrate to governmental leaders that the group still has the capacity to disrupt the system.[63]

After years of frustration, the black community has relied on violence to an increasing extent as an alternative route for airing their grievances. Coser, in reviewing the consequences of the Watts riot in 1965, comments: "The riot appears to have stemmed, at least in part, from frustrated efforts of the community to call attention to its plight. It seems to have been a cry for help . . . where other means to draw attention to the community's distress seemed socially unavailable." [64]

OTHER CONFLICT RESOURCES. Kenneth Gergen has identified other aspects of issue conflicts that bear on agenda-building. He asserts that "subphase resources" are important determinants of the likelihood of success in disputes. Included under this heading are initiation, staffing and planning, communication and publicity, institutional sanction, financing, and sanction and control. Gergen assumes that the more a group can optimize the above resources, the greater its chances of expanding an issue. He suggests that "personal efficacy" is another important intervening element.[65] Those whose per-

---

[63] H. L. Nieburg, "The Threat of Violence and Social Change," *American Political Science Review* 56 (1962), pp. 865–73.

[64] Lewis Coser, *Study of Social Conflict,* p. 101. For a general review of the role of violence in helping groups gain system access, see Chapters 3–5.

[65] The assumption that more of these resources will serve to publicize the conflict needs no basic elaboration. Gergen asserts that he who "initiates" the controversy might have the initial advantage of defining the conflict. For a review of the above elements and how they relate to the expansion of a conflict,

sonalities facilitate active commitment to a cause despite temporary obstacles will be an asset to a contending group. Finally, he specifies that system size is relevant, because the number of leverage points will increase as the system grows.

The Language of Conflict and Agenda-Building

One other aspect of conflict bears on the problem of agenda-building. That is the language, or the types of symbols, employed by conflicting parties to gain the attention of possible allies. A symbol such as "Black Power" can be an important rallying cry and may serve as a catalyst in helping a group muster the support necessary to command attention.

The problem of the utilization of language has long been a concern of disciplines other than political science. Writing on the role of symbols more than three decades ago, Edward Sapir stated:

> The term . . . covers a great variety of apparently dissimilar modes of behavior. . . . [It] is always a substitute for some more closely intermediating type of behavior, whence it follows that all symbolism implies meanings which cannot be derived directly from the contexts of experience . . . its actual significance being out of all proportion to the apparent triviality of meaning suggested by its mere form.[66]

Sapir differentiates between two types of symbols, noting that some symbols have factual referents (for example, accident statistics) while others have emotive bases. Most of the language of politics consists of the emotive types of cues. A typical political symbol "strikes deeper and deeper roots in the unconscious and diffuses its emotional quality to types of behavior or situations apparently far removed from the original meaning of the symbol." [67]

Two decades ago, a linguist, Charles Morris, developed an elaborate scheme for classifying different types of language used in various

---

see Kenneth Gergen, "Assessing the Leverage Points in the Process of Policy Formation," in Raymond Bauer and Kenneth Gergen (eds.), *The Study of Policy Formation* (New York: Free Press, 1968), pp. 183–93.

[66] Edward Sapir, "Symbolism," *Encyclopedia of the Social Sciences* 14 (1934), pp. 492–93.

[67] *Ibid.*, p. 494.

situations. He differentiated sixteen types of contexts, of which "political discourse" was one. He asserted that such a language tends to be valuative and prescriptive. It tends to make judgments about particular standards of behavior without providing information or factual statements to support various contentions. Political language is directed toward achieving a particular form of organization designed to implement various belief positions.[68]

SYMBOLIC USAGE IN BUILDING AGENDAS. Murray Edelman was among the first political scientists to utilize Sapir's scheme and show its political ramifications. His contributions to the study of agenda-building fall into three main areas: the utilization of symbols as placebos for various subgroups within the populace; the importance of leadership styles in coping with issues; and the types of language used in various political contexts.[69]

Edelman differentiates between referential symbols (those with a factual basis) and condensational symbols (those with an emotive base). He notes that a government has a limited number of tangible rewards, such as jobs, programs, and money, that it can dole out to various groups. Highly organized, cohesive groups tend to garner most of the available tangible rewards. To the remainder of the population, the government dispenses symbolic rewards. The public is reassured and quiescence is promoted by the utilization of condensation symbols like "the American way," "the national interest," and "the general welfare." Decision-makers help to determine which issues will receive formal agenda access by manipulating such symbols.

However, group leaders may also use condensation symbols to bring satellite groups to their cause, promoting the chances of their demands gaining access to the systemic agenda and thus to some specific institutional agenda. One of the most successful symbolic techniques, according to Edelman, is to create an enemy. One of the most commonly used enemies that evokes a strong public response is communism. Thus, it is not surprising that groups argue that the "communist conspiracy" can be found in such diversified places as the State Department and the local library. One of the reasons why the American Medical Association was able to keep Medicare off

[68] Charles Morris, *Signs, Language and Behavior* (New York: George Braziller, 1946), p. 125; 145–46.
[69] Edelman, *op. cit.*, passim.

the formal agenda for such a long time despite widespread public support was that the association used the symbol *socialized medicine*. This conjured up all types of emotional feelings, anxieties, and hatreds. As a consequence, governmental participation in health programs was put off for nearly two decades.

Edelman identifies another important facet of leadership that will be critical to a group trying to get its issue or concern onto a governmental agenda. Leaders must create the impression that they are acting decisively whether or not it is actually the case. They must utilize symbols and language to give the impression that they are effectively coping with problems. The usage of phrases like "was in consultation with" or "will meet with governmental leaders today" gives the impression to followers and possible ancillary groups that the leadership is making progress in getting their issue before the proper authorities.[70]

Edelman also stresses the importance of language to suit the occasion and notes that types of language:

> fall into a rather small number of patterns . . . and the most important conclusions are those about which we can be the most confident: that [language] style does convey meaning and that the meaning is a central explanation of political stability or polarization. . . . The use of particular language styles is a more sensitive and useful index of political functions . . . than conventional divisions . . . [of] actions.[71]

Edelman distinguishes between several types of language. *Hortatory* language is used to exhort one's followers to greater efforts on behalf of his cause. As Edelman notes, "Popular semantic analysis concentrates on the terms commonly employed in hortatory language such as 'democracy,' 'communism,' 'justice,' and the 'public interest,' and nothing is easier than to show that people read different meanings into them."[72]

As a consequence, when leaders of particular causes want to enlist outside support to enlarge the conflict, they tend to rely on hortatory language. However, as Edelman observes, "the most effective

[70] See Edelman, *op. cit.*, pp. 78–79.
[71] *Ibid.*, pp. 133–34.
[72] *Ibid.*, p. 134.

strategy is to conceal emotional appeal under the guise of defining issues." [73]

Another type of language is *bargaining,* which is used in an attempt to obtain an agreement with the opposing party. The emphasis is on stressing common interests rather than divisive aspects of the conflict. Thus, both sides might agree that the issue is important enough to be placed on the formal agenda. However, as Edelman reflects, this type of action is normally confined to private meetings and is often part of an overall ritual. [74]

A further distinction may be made between competitive and cooperative bargaining situations. In the former, symbolic language is often used to conceal the action priorities and preferences of the protagonists. Condensation symbols are indispensable, since they legitimate each side to a larger public but do not reveal the contents of either side's objectives. In the cooperative bargaining situations, on the other hand, language is used to communicate priorities and to reveal preferences to one another.

Edelman presents only one aspect of symbol impact on spectators. Language can be used not only to promote quiescence, but also to bring a response from people who had remained apathetic in the past. For example, symbols are utilized to activate people in elections and issue campaigns. In a study of the reform campaign in St. Louis, Robert Salisbury has noted the importance of symbols in activating sub-groups:

> On both sides the concern for concrete objectives was gradually superseded by concern for the slogans of a quasi-class struggle. The concepts of reform easily led to the use of such symbols as "decay," "party bosses," "power-hungry labor leaders," and assorted other "selfish interests" against whom reform campaigns have been directed for more than half a century. The assaults on the values and integrity of charter opponents evoked responses in kind. [75]

[73] *Ibid.,* p. 137.
[74] The other types of language are *legal* and *administrative,* which refer to what happens to an issue once it achieves agenda recognition and is transformed into law. For that reason, they are excluded from the above discussion. For a review of Edelman's arguments, see *Ibid.,* chapters 2, 4 and 7.
[75] Robert Salisbury, "The Dynamics of Reform: Charter Politics in St. Louis," *Midwest Journal of Political Science* 5 (1961), p. 273. For a general review of an election involving symbols leading to an active, not a quiescent, response see *Ibid.,* pp. 260–75.

LEGITIMACY, SYMBOL WEIGHT, AND AGENDA-BUILDING.   Richard Merelman has taken some of Edelman's notions and tried to specify further ramifications of the systemic reliance on symbols. He asserts that the key set of symbols undergirding any system relates to the notion of legitimacy. Therefore, to obtain access to the systemic agenda, groups must utilize such symbols in their public appeals for support. He writes:

> Policy-makers attempt to associate the symbols of legitimacy with policies that they wish implemented. By imposing symbols of legitimacy on such policies, they associate them with the material and symbolic rewards that motivate public compliance.[76]

In the conflict between groups to place issues on the systemic agenda, success will hinge on the use of available legitimacy symbols. Not only is it important to attach them to the issue, but it is also crucial to demonstrate that one's opponents have not tied legitimacy symbols to their stance. Merelman characterizes this twofold strategy as follows:

> Indeed, most major political conflicts within any polity may be seen as the attempt by partisans to attach the available legitimacy symbols to the policies they advocate and to sever the relationship between these symbols and the policies of their opponents.[77]

In addition to questioning the symbol sanctions of opponents, a group can use symbols to siphon off some of the opponent's support. In that instance, it bypasses the opposition's leadership to appeal directly to its members, asking them to reject their leadership.

In elaborating on Edelman's dichotomy of referential and condensational symbols, Merelman argues that there must be some differentiating criteria that can specify aspects of the language of politics in issue disputes. He introduces the notion of *symbol weight* and asserts that some symbols are intrinsically more powerful in bringing about a popular response.

He suggests that the following aspects of symbol weight can be delineated:

[76] Richard Merelman, "Learning and Legitimacy," *American Political Science Review* 60 (1966), p. 553.
[77] *Ibid.*

> the number of areas to which it [the symbol] can be applied, the intensity of the emotional response it provokes such that it encourages learning and compliance, the number of potential implementors among whom it evokes such a response, and the policy-implementing importance of the sub-groups among which it exercises power.[78]

Merelman suggests that weights could be calculated for each symbol, given such a list of indicators.[79] Thus, issue disputes that involve symbols with more weight tend to have greater agenda potential than controversies that do not exploit relevant symbols.

However, the symbol must be consonant with the particular issue being advocated. The weight of the symbol must be equal to the magnitude of the issue. If symbols of little weight are used to reinforce an important debate, there will be very little additional impact on possible supporters of the issue. On the other hand, if symbols of the greatest weight are used to back issues of narrower scope, then the symbols will be cheapened and in the future other symbols will have to be found to endorse specific policies.

Merelman also argues that certain symbols are timeless in that they have application over a long period of time (e.g., *Americanism* and *liberty*), but other symbols have a temporal limitation. Groups that seek recognition must utilize current symbols; otherwise, their issue will not be widely publicized. For example, a decade ago *law and order* was not a symbol capable of inciting a tremendous emotional response from the majority of the populace; today it is one of the most powerful.[80]

Another example of how symbols can change in strength with the passing of time concerns educational policy. Ten years ago *school bussing* was not a highly controversial symbol for most white parents. But when it appeared that civil rights groups would succeed in placing that issue on the formal agenda of local school boards, considerable opposition developed around a new symbol, the *neighbor-*

---

[78] *Ibid.*, p. 556.

[79] As far as empirical tests, he said, "We must take into account public opinion polls, the history of the symbol's development and previous application, and its relationship to projected uses." See *Ibid.*, p. 556.

[80] For a more thorough review of Merelman's notion of *symbol weight,* see *Ibid.*, pp. 554–57.

hood school. The bussing issue was thus denied formal agenda status in a number of cities.

One of the criticisms of the notion of symbol weight as advanced by Merelman is that the focus is on the type of emotional response a symbol will engender. However, what may be required is a notion of weight that is intrinsic to the symbol itself, such as number of issue areas that can lead to a particular type of response. Nonetheless, Merelman's arguments are clearly relevant to the study of agenda-building.

4

Cases in Agenda-Building

The study of agenda-building is concerned with the identification and specification of the types of issue conflict that receive the attention and action of governmental decision-makers. A central concern is to determine what type of conflict between small, involved parties gains mass recognition and leads to the demand for governmental action. In the process of enlarging the conflict over an issue, how does the issue change in what is at stake for both parties and outsiders? The key is to identify issues and survey why certain issues receive governmental attention and others seemingly of equal merit are ignored or bypassed by the decision-makers at all levels of government.

Most studies of issues focus on the dynamics of the conflict once an issue reaches the formal agenda in some form.[1] However, the study of the agenda-building process focuses on the issue conflict be-

[1] For examples of typical studies that focus on issues after they reach the agenda, see Theodore Draper, *The Dominican Revolt* (New York: Commentary Reports, 1968); and Louis Keonig, "Kennedy and Steel: The Great Price Dispute," in Alan Westin (ed.), *The Centers of Power: 3 Cases in American National Government* (New York: Harcourt, 1964), pp. 2–52. For examples of theoretical attempts to conceptualize the problem of issues after they reach the agenda, see Raymond Bauer and Kenneth Gergen (eds.), *The Study of Policy Formation* (New York: Free Press, 1968); and Yehezkel Dror, *Public Policymaking Reexamined* (San Francisco: Chandler, 1968).

fore it reaches the public docket. The object is to isolate those elements in the conflict that led to the expansion of the dispute beyond those initially involved.

Agenda-building has been of at least peripheral interest to political scientists over the past few decades. To illustrate how questions of issue development and expansion can be related to conflict within the context of an agenda-building perspective, let us analyze three case studies by first reviewing events and then reinterpreting them in terms of how issues come to receive formal agenda consideration. Two conflicts were taken from domestic policy, each illustrating a different type of path to an institutional agenda. A third example was drawn from foreign policy. A fourth case will be discussed to show that not all issues will necessarily gain access to either the formal or the systemic agenda. The selection of such issues was deliberate to show how questions of agenda-building transcend the nature of the issue or the type of governmental agency involved.

The Miners' Strike

The first case began with the cave-in of a West Virginia coal mine in late 1968. On November 20, an explosion at Consolidated Coal Company's No. 9 mine trapped seventy-eight miners below the surface. All of them died before they could be rescued. Prior to this incident, relatively little had been done about mine safety, even though mining was a notoriously hazardous occupation. As one correspondent wrote, "Knowledgeable people leave the impression that the mining safety record—the worst of any major industry—could indeed be better and the blame should indeed be spread widely." [2]

Despite frequent accidents, there had been no legislation enacted to regulate the industry since the 1952 Coal Mine Safety Act, which was neither harsh nor rigidly enforced. The only agency that had been given responsibility for miner protection was the Bureau of the Mines. However, criticism was levelled at it for being too "oriented to increasing production efficiency." [3] Critics also argued that

[2] Spencer Rich, "Mine-Safety Lag Conceded," *Washington Post,* December 8, 1968, p. B1.
[3] *Ibid.*, p. B10.

more frequent inspections were required to prevent mine disasters.

The tragedy of November 20 served as a catalyst in bringing a raft of mining problems to the fore. They included not only mine collapses, but also black lung disease, a miners' disease caused by inhaling coal dust. Faced with a lack of official concern, the miners, who were notoriously apathetic in the past, embarked on a strategy of collective action to demonstrate their dissatisfaction.

As the miners and public of West Virginia's mining towns became increasingly aroused, President Johnson requested that funds be included in the 1970 budget to improve mining safety.[4] However, the miners' demands for action did not center exclusively on the government. In late January, 1969, over 3,000 West Virginia miners attended a statewide meeting of the West Virginia Black Lung Association to demand that the United Mine Workers (the miners' union) as well as the federal government take action to improve health and safety standards.[5]

On February 20, more than 1,000 miners left their jobs to participate in a demonstration that they hoped would lead the West Virginia legislature to approve a bill providing for medical compensation for "black lung" victims. A dozen mines were affected by the walkout, and the miners asserted that if the legislature failed to act, they would march on the capitol in Charleston.[6]

Within the same week, wildcat strikes closed most of the mines in southern West Virginia with estimates of participants running over 12,000. Some representatives of the miners went to Charleston in an effort to persuade key legislators of the cruciality of their needs.[7] A state representative who supported the miners' grievances asserted that he did not "believe that endless, bitter and disorganized strikes and walkouts [would] solve the problem or result in good legislation." [8] Nonetheless, the movement of concerned miners con-

[4] "2.9 Million Asked For Safe Mine Plan," *New York Times,* January 16, 1969, p. 22.
[5] "Miners Organize To Reduce Risks," *New York Times,* January 27, 1969, p. 30.
[6] "1,000 Quit West Virginia Mines For 'Lung' Bill," *Washington Post,* February 20, 1969, p. A11.
[7] "12,000 Coal Miners Join Wildcat Strike," *New York Times,* February 24, 1969, p. 16.
[8] "Miners Weigh A 'Black Lung' March," *Washington Post,* February 22, 1969, p. A6.

tinued to spread, reaching into the mining areas of Kentucky and Pennsylvania.[9]

Faced with the legislature's hesitancy to act, more than 1,000 West Virginia miners marched on the state capitol on February 26 to demonstrate their support for remedial legislation. The miners overran state policemen barring their presence in House galleries and shouted down legislators who attempted to quiet them. Even the Governor came to the capitol to assure the miners that if the legislature did not act, he would propose a mine safety bill of his own. " 'No! No! No!,' the miners roared. 'Now! Now! Now!' " [10] State legislators responded that the chamber would put their grievances up for immediate consideration.

At the same time, the Labor Subcommittee of the United States Senate began holding hearings to see if there were ameliorative steps that might be taken at the federal level to help the miners. These initiatives were further bolstered by a threat of a nationwide strike by the United Mine Workers if reform legislation was not forthcoming. As a sign of further concern, President Nixon ordered a message on coal safety, as well as a specific bill, to be put before the Congress by early March. The bill that was subsequently introduced to reduce deaths from mine accidents and to protect miners from blacklung disease was even stronger than the one previously offered by President Johnson.[11]

In early March, the West Virginia legislature unanimously approved a compensation bill that was signed into law.[12] Even with victory, the miners continued to push for strong federal action on mine safety, repeatedly threatening a nationwide strike.[13] In early October, the United States Senate overwhelmingly approved a mine safety bill by a vote of 73 to 0.[14] The House of Representatives followed suit in

[9] "12,000 Coal Miners Join Wildcat Strike," p. 16.
[10] "Miners' Rally Wins Lung Aid," *Washington Post,* February 27, 1969, p. A4.
[11] "Grisly Statistics Prompt Senators To Open Hearings On Mine Safety," *Washington Post,* February 28, 1969, p. A2.
[12] " 'Blacklung' Bill Passed By West Virginia Senate," *New York Times,* March 6, 1969, p. 21.
[13] Ben Franklin, "Mine Strikes Predicted If Stiff Safety Bill Fails," *New York Times,* July 5, 1969, p. 10.
[14] "Senate 73-0, Approves Coal Mine Safety Bill," *New York Times,* October 3, 1969, p. 19.

late October.[15] On November 20, the bill cleared the conference committee, and the Federal Coal Mine and Safety Act of 1969 was sent to the President in mid-December despite his threat of a veto because of its cost.[16] Faced with the threat of a presidential veto, miners in Charleston, West Virginia, picketed to protest Nixon's hesitancy in signing the bill.[17] Within a day after the picketing had begun, the White House announced that the President would sign the bill despite his concern that the cost would prove inflationary. In signing the bill, the President proclaimed it "an historic advance in industry practices." [18]

The Grape Strike

A second issue conflict that is relevant to the problems of agenda-building concerns the grape workers in southern California. Grape pickers have generally been better paid than other farm workers, but their average yearly pay is between $2,200 and $2,400, or less than the $3,000 poverty level established by the federal government.[19] Among their grievances were no job security, no unemployment insurance, and no union. In late 1965, Cesar Chavez organized the farm workers into a rudimentary organization with sufficient cohesion to call a strike in Delano, a key area for grape production.

The strike soon obtained the support of other groups, and knowledge of the grape workers' cause spread beyond southern California. The Northern California Council of Churches aided in arousing the public and encouraging fencesitters to join the strike. The symbols for the strike became "La Huelga" and "La Causa." As one commentator wrote, the "group has been transformed from a Califor-

[15] Ben Franklin, "Mine Health And Safety Bill Is Passed By House, 389-4," *New York Times,* October 30, 1969, p. 1.
[16] Richard Lyons, "House Ignores Threat Of Veto To Pass Tough Mine Safety Bill," *Washington Post,* December 18, 1969, p. A3.
[17] "Miners' Strike To Support Safety Bill," *Washington Post,* December 29, 1969, p. A5.
[18] Don Oberdorfer, "Nixon To Sign Mine Bill Despite Some Misgivings," *Washington Post,* December 30, 1969, p. A1.
[19] Dick Meister, " 'La Huelga' Becomes 'La Causa,' " *The New York Times Magazine,* November 17, 1968, p. 82.

nia farm workers' strike into a civil rights [and] a quasi-religious cause." [20]

In March, 1966, 10,000 supporters thronged at the state capitol steps in Sacramento to demand, in the words of Cesar Chavez, "a new social order for the farm worker." [21] Some of the participants had marched 300 miles, from Delano to Sacramento, to draw attention to their cause.[22] Such efforts to publicize the strike led to groups outside of California joining the dispute. Walter Reuther, head of the United Auto Workers, pledged to donate $5,000 a month for the duration of the strike. The American Federation of Labor-Congress of Industrial Organizations sent a director of organization to Delano full-time, with a monthly budget of $10,000. Outside contributions approached a quarter of a million dollars.[23]

The strike attracted participants who wanted to contribute more than money. Civil rights groups identified the cause of the grape workers with that of other downtrodden groups in society.

> "I am here," announced an early arrival in clerical garb, "because this is a movement by the poor people themselves to improve their position, and where the poor people are, Christ should be and is." Other supporters . . . said much the same thing in their own way: This was part of their own battle against society's power structure.[24]

Other actions gave the cause nationwide publicity. They included a national boycott of table grapes, the support of candidates for the 1968 Democratic Presidential nomination, and fasts by Chavez. The boycott was particularly important. As Chavez noted, "It was the only way we could do it—take on the whole industry. . . . The grape itself had to become a label." [25] The boycott led large universities to cut their grape purchases. Protestants, Catholics, and Jews urged their members to stop buying grapes. By the summer of 1968, grape sales had dropped by 90 percent in New York, a state whose consumption accounted for one-fifth of the national market.[26]

However, the grape growers began to feel the threat of the

[20] *Ibid.*
[21] *Ibid.*, p. 94.
[22] *Ibid.*
[23] *Ibid.*, p. 96.
[24] *Ibid.*, p. 92.
[25] *Ibid.*, p. 109.
[26] *Ibid.*, p. 110.

strike and organized a counterattack. Newspaper and television documentaries focused on their side of the issue. The growers' arguments were tailored for the national public. First, they pictured grapes as a risky business, with taxes, equipment innovations, crop failures, and growing costs keeping profits at a minimum. Second, they stated that they were willing to sit down with any "reasonable union." However, the Chavez group did not qualify. In the words of one grower, "It's a rebel outfit that doesn't represent anybody." [27] Third, the owners stressed the benefits that the workers receive such as free transportation, housing, and the equivalent of over $2.10 an hour depending upon the quantity of grapes one picked. Fourth, they asserted that settling with such a union could drive the price of grapes up for the consumer. As one grape owner noted, "The consumer had better look out." [28]

In addition to such appeals for public support, the growers filed suits against the union seeking legal relief from the strike. Richard Nixon, while running for the Presidency, supported the owners and was pictured eating a bunch of grapes. A public relations campaign was launched stressing such themes as: "Feel better in all respects by buying and enjoying fresh California grapes." [29] The owners also attempted to influence other business organizations and the press to put their position in a favorable perspective. The California Farm Bureau Federation suggested that the boycott was creating a crisis in farm laborer relations, asserting that the nationwide attempt to ban grapes from homes is "one of the greatest threats ever to face our state's agriculture." [30]

By the spring of 1968, Chavez had settled with several growers producing wine grapes. Major facets of the settlement included a new minimum wage of $1.75 an hour, no strikes or lockouts, a union hiring hall, a union shop, pay for reporting, and paid vacations.[31] After this success, Chavez concentrated on forcing table grape growers to require workers to join a union. California grape pickers continued to strike all growers who refused the unionization of pickers, and Chavez sought to extend and intensify the nationwide boycott of table grapes.

[27] *Ibid.*, p. 111.
[28] *Ibid.*
[29] *Ibid.*, p. 110.
[30] *Ibid.*
[31] "California Grape Boycott," *Transaction,* February, 1969, p. 6.

As the boycott became increasingly effective, more growers agreed to talk with the union. By the end of September, 1969, the sale of table grapes had declined 30 percent from the 1965 level when the strike began.[32] Even those groups opposed to the unionization of grape workers were willing to concede that the boycott was hurting some growers.[33] To further bolster the boycott, Chavez embarked on a nationwide tour during November to gain support for the union's activities.[34]

On April 1, 1970, Chavez's organization signed the first American labor contract covering table grape pickers with two major California growers. The contract was hailed as "a breakthrough (that) will serve as a pattern for others who wish to solve this prolonged dispute." [35] Despite this success, the union continued its boycott of nonunion grapes.

By the time the first table grapes bearing union labels were shipped to market, seven central California growers had signed contracts with the union.[36] By the end of June, thirty growers had come to terms with the union, with approximately one-fifth of all table grapes in California produced under union pacts.[37]

By the end of July, nearly two-thirds of all growers were under contract. Buoyed by success, Chavez declared that the union's achievements demonstrated that social justice can be achieved through nonviolent action.[38] Taking a less sanguine view, Governor Ronald Reagan found the union success "tragic" in that workers had no choice in determining if they would join the union.[39] Shortly thereafter, the boycott drew to a close, having brought all major growers to the bargaining table.

Chavez announced that he was going to continue his efforts to unionize farm workers, concentrating on lettuce pickers. In mid-Sep-

[32] "Pentagon Accused By Chavez For Rise In Grape Purchases," *New York Times,* September 29, 1969, p. 96.

[33] "Grape Grower Chief Derides Union Drive," *New York Times,* October 2, 1969, p. 47.

[34] Steven Roberts, "Grape Boycott: Struggle Poses A Moral Issue," *New York Times,* November 12, 1969, p. 49.

[35] Robert Wright, "Farm Workers' Union Signs First Table Grape Contract With Two California Growers," *New York Times,* April 2, 1970, p. 29.

[36] Steven Roberts, "First Grapes With Union Label Shipped To Market From Coast," *New York Times,* May 31, 1970, p. 56.

[37] "Union Signs Grape Growers," *New York Times,* June 30, 1970, p. 34.

[38] Steven Roberts, "26 Grape Growers Sign Union Accord: Boycott Nears End," *New York Times,* July 30, 1970, p. 1.

[39] "Reagan Issues Statement," *New York Times,* July 30, 1970, p. 19.

tember, he called for a nationwide boycott of all lettuce not bearing his union's label. Despite strong opposition, Chavez has resolved to continue the struggle.[40]

While Chavez has concentrated his efforts in California, success in the movement has led to increased attempts to unionize farm workers in other areas. Efforts to organize in Florida, Texas, and Wisconsin can be traced to the success of Chavez in southern California.[41] There can be little doubt that Chavez's efforts have been a spur to federal government action. Although Congress failed to complete action on a bill extending coverage of the National Labor Relations Act to farm workers in 1968, both House and Senate Committees have conducted hearings and have reported bills favorable to farm workers.[42] It seems likely that legislation will ultimately be passed extending minimum wage and unemployment protection to all farm workers and guaranteeing their right to organize. Those gains will owe much to the struggle of the California grape pickers.

As one commentator has noted, Chavez's organization "was the first agricultural union to obtain recognition and contracts with major employers through a strike. An important fact was public support. . . ."[43] The mobilization of public support was in part due to the type of language and symbols used by Chavez and his supporters during the strike. The language was both colorful and emotional, including remnants from the civil rights movement such as "we shall overcome" and its Spanish equivalent of "nosotros venceremos." Terms such as *La Huelga* and *La Causa* were commonplace. Boycott organizers peppered their statements with words and phrases such as *nonviolence, struggle, there's no turning back now, they destroy our union or we destroy them, strike,* and *boycott.*[44]

The Decision to Reconsider
the Anti-Ballistic Missile System

A third case involving the placing of a dispute on an institutional agenda concerns foreign policy. Over the past few years, there has

[40] "Chavez Calls Lettuce Boycott," *New York Times,* September 18, 1970, 11.
[41] Irving Cohen, "La Huelga, Delano And After," *Monthly Labor Review* 91 No. 6 (June, 1968), p. 15.
[42] *Congressional Quarterly Almanac. 90th Congress, 2nd Session, 1968. Volume XXIV.* Washington, D.C.: Congressional Quarterly, 1968.
[43] Cohen, *op. cit.,* p. 16.
[44] Meister, *op. cit.,* p. 114.

been much consideration given to the development and deployment of an anti-ballistic missile system (ABM) that would effectively deter either a Chinese or a Soviet threat. When the matter was initially raised by the Defense Department, knowledgeable observers assumed that any official military recommendation would be accepted with little public outcry and a minimal negative reaction in the Congress.

Leading Pentagon spokesmen have long harped on the idea that the United States has lagged in the development of a defensive missile system that could cope with an enemy attack. Major officials in the military bureaucracy "have long been hammering at the theme that the Soviets are outspending the United States in both offensive and defensive strategic weapons." [45]

The reaction of the residents of Libertyville, Illinois, was typical of the larger public response. Libertyville is a rather conservative town of about 10,000 people with a $13,100 median family income. In November, 1968, the United States Army announced that it was considering Libertyville as one of five possible sites near Chicago for the installation of a Sentinel ABM. Initially, this announcement provoked little more than a ripple of concern. Most of the comment centered on the economic impact of the project. Mayor Charles Brown told a reporter that the site "will do nothing but good for the economy of the area. This site has to be established somewhere, so why not here?" [46]

However, after the announcement, some opposition began to crystallize on the basis of one or more of the following reasons: the Sentinel might be unsafe and explode; the deployment of the system might make the area a prime target for the enemy; and there are better uses for the money. However, the issue remained fairly muted until fourteen prominent clergymen issued a statement opposing the installation of the system on moral grounds. These clergymen included the most conservative churchmen in the area, who had never before taken a stance on a social issue.[47]

Once the clergy issued a statement, the Village Board decided not to take a public position other than urging citizens to make their

[45] George Ashworth, "Pentagon Talks Up ABM Revision," *Washington Post,* March 4, 1969, p. A7.
[46] Ward Just, "Siting The ABM: A Town Reacts," *Washington Post,* February 27, 1969, p. A20.
[47] *Ibid.*

opinions known "to our representatives in Washington." [48] Shortly thereafter, a new group, called the Northern Illinois Citizens Against the ABM, became prominent in its opposition to the proposed deployment of the system. It released propaganda to the local press that played on such themes as: "If you live in Libertyville [and surrounding areas] . . . and an accidental explosion occurred, your house would be leveled, your property would be consumed by fire, and your children would be burned to death." [49]

Seeing that opposition was building in one community and that it might spill over into other areas, the Army sent two colonels to Libertyville "with charts and bar graphs with them to explain the importance of the ABM." [50] A public meeting was held with representatives from both the military and opposition groups. The Pentagon officials stressed such themes as the *communist threat* and a *credible deterrent* and asserted that such a program was needed to counteract a similar undertaking by the Soviet Union.

However, opponents of the program were able to capitalize on public fears of nuclear attack and accident to create a public furor in Libertyville. Senator Charles Percy and the congressman from the area were deluged with letters on the ABM, most of them opposing the project.[51] In addition, the Northern Illinois group instituted a lawsuit which charged that the area had been denied due process when the government failed to stipulate the locations in the authorizing legislation. The government's attorneys sought to have the suit thrown out of court. However, the trial judge asserted that the case must be heard.

> There must be some point where executive insanity can be stopped. Don't tell me that every time a government official acts, he's immune from prosecution unless he consents to be sued.[52]

Similar reactions developed in other areas from Honolulu to Detroit and Boston, with a number of indignant citizens writing letters to congressmen protesting the system's penetration of their re-

[48] *Ibid.*
[49] Ward Just, "Citizens' Dilemma Over The ABM," *Washington Post,* February 23, 1969, p. A22.
[50] *Ibid.*
[51] Just, "Citizens' Dilemma Over the ABM," p. A22.
[52] "Illinois ABM Foes Win First Round," *Washington Post,* March 5, 1969, p. A2.

spective areas.[53] As a consequence, key legislators asserted that Sentinel's deployment must be reconsidered. Senator Stuart Symington, long a friend of the armed forces, asserted that the ABM system might cost as much as $400 billion, or "more than the current national debt." [54] Mike Mansfield, the majority leader of the Senate, asserted that the ABM "is in trouble, as far as the Senate is concerned. . . . The future of the ABM is in doubt." [55]

The governmental spokesmen announced that the critics of the Sentinel had forced a reconsideration of the entire issue. Military leaders said they were already thinking of alternative strategies for rewriting the legislation prior to bringing it up before Congress. Pentagon spokesmen suggested revising the program to shift the system away from populated areas and increase protection of Minuteman missile sites.[56] In March, 1969, President Nixon announced that he would seek Congressional approval of a modified ABM system that he called "Safeguard." Although essentially the same system, its purpose had shifted from protection of cities to the protection of the American deterrent.

Secretary of Defense Laird asserted that this modified system would be a building block to peace, would protect the American deterrent, and would not escalate the arms race.[57] Senator Fulbright, however, accused Laird of invoking fear of the Soviet Union to promote the Safeguard system.[58] Senator Mansfield said that testimony indicated that the Safeguard system was merely the first step of a vast program to convert the nation into a "missile Maginot." [59]

Outside of Congress, 3,200 scientists and scholars signed an open letter asking President Nixon to abandon Safeguard.[60] A non-

[53] Marquis Childs, "There's Trouble in Paradise: ABM Plan Stirs Hawaiians," *Washington Post,* February 28, 1969, p. A23.
[54] "Senate Critics of ABM Hit Costs, Urban Sites," *Washington Post,* March 5, 1969, p. A2.
[55] Godfrey Sperling, "Mansfield Objects To Timing Of ABM Projects," *Christian Science Monitor,* February 28, 1969, p. 7.
[56] Ashworth, *op. cit.,* p. 7.
[57] "Sentinel Backed By Laird As Vital To Thwart Soviet," *New York Times,* March 21, 1969, p. 1.
[58] "Fulbright Says Laird Uses Fear To Promote ABM," *New York Times,* March 22, 1969, p. 1.
[59] "Mansfield Criticizes Pentagon On Its ABM Views," *New York Times,* March 25, 1969, p. 14.
[60] "3200 Scholars Ask Half On Safeguard," *New York Times,* March 23, 1969, p. 35.

partisan coalition of eminent citizens was formed to oppose Safeguard.[61] Mayor John Lindsay of New York City questioned large outlays for the system in light of pressing city needs.[62] While the public debate raged, a Gallup poll reported that as of the first week in April, only 40 percent of the population had formed an opinion on the issue, with 25 percent favoring deployment.[63]

Faced with mounting opposition to the ABM system, President Nixon appointed New York Governor Nelson Rockefeller to head a nonpartisan review board to advise him on the suitability of the Safeguard system. This board ultimately supported the President's position.[64] Rogers Morton, chairman of the National Committee of the Republican Party, asserted that the Safeguard had become a partisan issue and planned an elaborate campaign to win additional support for the system.[65]

The controversy raged through the months of April and May. In late April, twenty-six prominent churchmen signed a statement announcing the formation of the National Religious Committee Opposing ABM. Nonetheless, popular sentiment for Safeguard seemed to be growing. A Harris poll of late April showed almost twice as many for the system as against it.[66] In early May, a meeting of 1,216 scientists at the American Physical Society produced a poll showing that 76 percent of those present opposed Safeguard.[67] But a week later, Vice-President Agnew contended that the "responsible majority in the scientific community" [68] believes in the workability of Safeguard.

The first legislative vote on AMB occurred near the end of

---

[61] "A New Coalition Will Oppose ABM," *New York Times,* March 30, 1969, p. 26.
[62] Martin Tolchin, "Negro Minister Applauds Lindsay's Courage Before Conference in Harlem," *New York Times,* April 8, 1969, p. 37.
[63] "Gallup Poll Finds Support For ABM," *New York Times,* April 6, 1969, p. 35.
[64] "Rockefeller Named Adviser to Nixon," *New York Times,* March 21, 1969, p. 20.
[65] William Chapman, "Senate ABM Foes Decry Partisanship," *Washington Post,* April 15, 1969, p. A4.
[66] "Churchmen Score The Missile System And Nixon's Views," *New York Times,* April 30, 1969, p. 9.
[67] "Poll of 1216 Physicists Find 76% Against ABM System," *New York Times,* May 1, 1969, p. 21.
[68] "Agnew Says Foes of ABM Are Weak In Their Criticism," *New York Times,* May 8, 1969, p. 10.

June. The Senate Armed Services Committee approved the system by a vote of 10 to 7. Senator Stuart Symington, noting the sharp split, said that it was the first time in his seventeen years on the committee that there had ever been such division.[69] When the bill reached the Senate floor, the debate became highly emotional. Supporters of the Safeguard system asserted that opponents would lead the United States "down the road to a Munich" with the Soviet Union.[70] Opponents of the system argued that the Defense Department was withholding reports highly critical of the ABM.[71]

The Senate controversy seemed to increase popular doubts regarding the Safeguard system. By the end of July, Gallup reported that 23 percent of the population supported the Safeguard system, 18 percent opposed it, and the remainder were undecided or unaware. This poll reflected a slight rise in opposition over earlier polls.[72]

On August 7, the Senate approved the Safeguard plan by a vote of 51 to 50.[73] Shortly thereafter, the House approved the deployment of the system by a vote of 219 to 105.[74] While the closeness of the Senate vote was hailed by some as a moral victory for the opponents of growing military expenditures, the whole issue attracted relatively little attention when further appropriations were requested in 1970 to expand the system. Extension of the Safeguard system passed both the House and Senate with larger victory margins than expected and relatively little public controversy.[75]

When the Sentinel-Safeguard system was first proposed, its advocates hardly expected the controversy that ensued. Matters of public policy relating to national security normally receive only token attention and little opposition. However, the strong public reaction

[69] "Senate Unit Votes Safeguard 10-7, Heralding Fight," *New York Times,* June 28, 1969, p. 1.

[70] John Finney, "ABM Fight Taken To Senate Floor," *New York Times,* July 24, 1969, p. 1.

[71] John Finney, "A Senate Dispute Blocks ABM Vote," *New York Times,* July 29, 1969, p. 5.

[72] "Poll Shows Most Unsure Over ABM," *New York Times,* July 27, 1969, p. 27.

[73] Warren Weaver, "Nixon Missile Plan Wins In Senate By 51-50 Vote, House Approval Likely," *New York Times,* August 7, 1969, p. 1.

[74] Marjorie Hunter, "House Turns Back Effort To Block ABM Deployment," *New York Times,* October 3, 1969, p. 1.

[75] John Finney, "Expansion Of ABM Backed By Senate By 52-To-47 Vote," *New York Times,* August 13, 1970, p. 1.

against the system forced the decision-makers to reconsider their position and to offer a new proposal for institutional consideration.

Review of Case Studies in Context of Agenda Creation

Given these three sequences of events, what can be said about them in the context of a study of governmental agenda-building? The agenda-building perspective leads us to ask the following:

1. How did the original disputants define each of these conflicts?
2. How were the conflicts enlarged to different subgroups within the population?
3. What types of symbols were used to add emotive connotations to the issue?
4. How did the setting in which these issues were fought help lead to the resolution of the conflict?
5. What characteristics of issues are the most salient for predicting how they might ultimately be resolved?

To illustrate the possible answers to the above questions, let us briefly review the three cases. In the coal mining disaster, a cave-in precipitated the conflict. After the cave-in, the miners organized, their initial issue being safety conditions in the mine to prevent future cave-ins. However, in an effort to publicize the conflict, the miners soon made the issue more emotional by stressing "black lung" disease. To dramatize their cause, they staged strikes and demonstrations that ultimately involved a great portion of the miners. Through their actions, the miners clearly and quickly succeeded in elevating their grievances to systemic agenda status.

In addition, the miners insisted on some type of response. Utilizing symbols such as *action now,* they made it difficult for the West Virginia legislators to avoid the issue. Thus, with issue redefinition, public protest, and action language, they were able to force the issue onto the formal agenda of the West Virginia state legislature and Congress.

In the case of the grape strike, the issue was handled slightly differently. The first step was to expand the issue to encompass a larger constituency than was initially involved. Instead of a farm dispute, the conflict was recast as a civil rights struggle involving the rights of an oppressed group, an item of long-standing on the systemic agenda of the American political community. This redefinition brought outside support from other unions, civil rights workers, etc. Expanding the issue to other farm workers (as the West Virginia miners expanded their issue) would not have been sufficient, since farm workers did not represent a potent political group in the state. Therefore, the grape pickers attempted to involve a constituency outside of California by appealing to the conscience of the nation. Their leaders made symbolic appeals, using terms such as *La Huelga* and implying that their cause involved a significant social protest that all "liberals" must support. Thus, their case received attention on the systemic agenda of political controversy.

Another key action toward activating a large populace was the boycott, which meant that every person could contribute to the effort by not buying grapes. The conflict received further national publicity when Chavez persuaded all leading Democratic Presidential candidates to take a public stance favorable to the strike.

The strike fostered formal agenda access for a number of farm worker grievances, although there is yet to be a definitive response from federal decision-makers. While ameliorative action seems likely, it is also quite possible that such action will include provisions to preclude further strikes. Thus, an item can be placed on a formal agenda with no assurance that the results will be uniformly positive. They may even be negative. Often, by the time an item reaches the institutional agenda, it may lose its potency on the systemic agenda, perhaps being redefined as an "illegal action" or an "arrogant power grab." [76]

Chavez's efforts to organize grape workers also illustrate another important aspect of the agenda-building process. His success with grape workers did not still his demands, but rather led him to make new demands (for example, the unionization of lettuce workers). His mission was no longer restricted to grape pickers, but focused on organization of all farm workers. This example thus serves to support Edelman's argument that "success in achieving a political objective leads to demands for . . . new goals different in manifest

[76] For a review of the owners' complaints, see Meister, *op. cit.*, pp. 99, 101 and 104.

content but like the old ones in respect to a latent dimension." [77]

In the third instance, involving the anti-ballistic missile system, another type of agenda item was created. Not only was foreign policy involved, but the government placed the item on the formal agenda in the first place by passing an appropriation for a study program. The reconsideration of the ABM issue was never anticipated by the governmental officials involved with the program. As a result, the re-evaluation of the program was forced upon unwilling decision-makers by a redefinition of the issue in terms of a new set of systemic agenda items.

Initially, the issue was defined as an appropriate military response to a Soviet or Chinese threat. However, opposition developed, and the issue was redefined as one of "safety" and "morality." When the new issue was publicized, many citizens in areas where no protest had been raised before were activated to write to their congressmen protesting the installation of the system.

In this situation, the opposition used key symbols such as *burning bodies* and other products of a nuclear holocaust. The coming of Pentagon representatives to the locations of potential base sites may have worked to the aid of the opposition, who were more familiar with the fears and values of local citizens. The local setting worked against the military by further arousing dissent rather than placating angry citizens. If the hearings were confined to Washington, there would have been greater likelihood of success in stifling opposition to the program.[78]

It is interesting that while many of the most stinging criticisms of the ABM system have centered on its technical feasibility, little was made of that in the public controversy. The administration's ploys of redefining the system's purpose and renaming it are also noteworthy. Once the Sentinel system (i.e., the city-centered ABM network) began to fall into public disfavor, the purpose of the proposed system was shifted from the protection of major population centers to the protection of the American missile deterrent. The system was no longer to be called "Sentinel," but was now a "Safeguard" system, a name that tended to reassure the public of both its propriety and importance.

---

[77] Murray Edelman, *The Symbolic Uses of Politics* (Urbana: University of Illinois Press, 1964), p. 153.
[78] Just, "Citizens' Dilemma Over the ABM," p. A22.

The ABM case demonstrates the importance of creating an enemy and manipulating him to suit your own ends. The military attempted this by using the *communist menace* as the enemy. This was the rationale behind the military position of "If the Russians have X, we must have one too."

The ABM case also illustrates another important facet of agenda-building. Once an item attains formal agenda access and is supported by even the narrowest margin, it is very difficult for opponents to preclude the item from subsequent agendas or to mobilize opposition when it appears again, often in expanded or extended form.

A Counter-example

Some public issues, however, have not attained access to either a formal or a systemic agenda. An interesting example of such an issue is the recurring demand to repeal the federal income tax. The whole question is historically highly emotional. In fact, perhaps the most serious threat to confront the United States as a fledgling nation arose over the issue of taxation (viz., Shays Rebellion of 1786–1788). It was this issue that led to the demise of the confederation and served as a catalyst toward the creation of the federal union. Thus, it is somewhat surprising that the demand to repeal the income tax has met with so little success.

With few exceptions, such as the Liberty League during the late 1930's, efforts to mobilize people around the issue have enjoyed little success. Some people continue to argue that the income tax is the root of all evil.

> It [the Sixteenth Amendment] corroded the American concept of natural right, reduced the American citizen to the status of a subject, enhanced executive power to the point of reducing Congress . . . into subservience.[79]

To members of the radical right, the tax is a salient symbol. With them, "the income tax . . . has been upgraded to become al-

[79] William Henry Chamberlain, "The Income Tax: Root of all Evil," *American Mercury* (August, 1954), p. 95.

most the central symbol of evil (i.e., the first entering wedge of communism)." [80]

Thus, even using such a potent symbol as *communism* to promote concern, the demand for repeal has attracted little public attention, arousing few people, and not convincing many that it is even a legitimate concern. In other words, the repeal effort has been unable to transform its demand into an item on the systemic agenda. At most, the repeal effort has succeeded in attaining only pseudo-agenda standing through the nominal introduction of periodic bills calling for revision of the Constitution. Unless it achieves systemic agenda status, it is highly unlikely that this demand will ever command a place on any formal agenda. In the absence of widespread corruption and inefficiency in the collection of taxes and with popular acceptance of the expanding range of governmental activities and responsibilities, it seems unlikely that the repeal demand will ever capture sufficient support to attain systemic agenda standing.

Summing Up

From the review of the foregoing case studies, it would seem that a perspective could be developed that could cut across a wide variety of both foreign and domestic issues. This might allow for the development of some generalizations about the genesis of agenda items. The key is to pass beyond descriptive interpretations of case studies and to develop some type of framework in which other case studies or aggregates can be used to verify or disconfirm propositions.

Instead of trying to debate the merits of a conflict in terms of which side has the "best" or more persuasive argument, the agenda-building perspective would focus on the way issues become defined initially and how they become reinterpreted over time. The techniques that issue leaders use to gain victory for their group would be examined. If the findings are relevant under these headings, comments would be in order about domestic or foreign issues.

[80] Talcott Parsons, "Social Strains in America: A Postscript," in Daniel Bell (ed.), *The Radical Right* (Garden City, New York: Doubleday, 1963), p. 235.

5

Issue Creation and Agenda Content

The literature and case studies reviewed in the previous chapters demonstrated that issue creation and agenda-building are key components of the larger process of public policy development. This chapter defines *issue* and various types of political agendas more specifically. Discussion centers on some of the precipitating elements that lead to the creation of public policy issues and the likely content of any specific institutional agenda. Finally, consideration is given to some of the institutional and structural factors that affect agenda content.

What Is an Issue? What Makes an Issue?

An issue is a conflict between two or more identifiable groups over procedural or substantive matters relating to the distribution of positions or resources. Generally, there are four means by which issues are created. The most common method is the manufacturing of an issue by one or more of the contending parties who perceive an unfavorable bias in the distribution of positions or resources. For example, in 1950 truckers in Pennsylvania thought the railroads had an inherent advantage in carrying freight over long distances and sought to create an issue to redress this imbalance.[1] Such initiators are labeled "readjustors."

Another form of issue creation can be traced to a person or group who manufacture an issue for their own gain; for example, individuals who want to run for public office and are looking for an issue to advance their cause. Such individuals may be labeled "exploiters." As Herbert Blumer has written:

> The gaining of sympathizers or members rarely occurs through a mere combination of a pre-established appeal and a pre-established individual psychological bent on which it is brought to bear. Instead the prospective sympathizer has to be aroused, nurtured and directed.[2]

Hans Toch echoes a similar sentiment when he writes:

> People are brought into social movements through the skills of leaders and agitators rather than because of pre-existing problems. . . . Appeals seem to originate with people who are primarily interested in other ends than the solution of the problems of potential members.[3]

Another means of issue initiation is through an unanticipated event. Such events could be called "circumstantial reactors." Examples include the development of an oil slick off the California coast near Santa Barbara in early 1969 that led to a reconsideration of the whole question of offshore drilling regulations. Other examples are the assassination of President Kennedy, which led to the gun control issue, and Eisenhower's heart attack in the mid-1950's, which raised the question of presidential disability.

Issues can be generated by persons or groups who have no positions or resources to gain for themselves. Often, they merely acquire a psychological sense of well-being for doing what they believe is in the public interest. These initiators might be called "do-gooders."

[1] For a case study of this conflict, see Andrew Hacker, "Pressure Politics in Pennsylvania: The Truckers vs. The Railroads," in Alan Westin (ed.), *The Uses of Power: 7 Cases in American Politics* (New York: Harcourt, 1962), pp. 323–76.
[2] Herbert Blumer, "Collective Behavior," in J. B. Gittler (ed.), *Review of Sociology* (New York: Wiley, 1957), 148.
[3] Hans Toch, *The Psychology of Social Movements* (Indianapolis: Bobbs-Merrill, 1965), 87.

The efforts to support Biafran relief programs fall in this category.

The above categories are not mutually exclusive, as an individual or group may have more than one motive for a particular action. For example, some people supported civil rights legislation because they felt it was humanitarian, while others supported it because they sought personal or collective gains.

TRIGGERING DEVICES.   At least two classes of triggering mechanisms, or unforeseen events, help shape issues that will be defined by the initiators. These can be subdivided into internal and external events that correspond to the domestic and foreign spheres.

Within the internal subdivision, there are five types of triggering devices. The first is a natural catastrophe, such as a mine cave-in, air inversion, flooding, and fire. The second is an unanticipated human event, such as a spontaneous riot, assassination of public officials, air hijackings, and murder of private individuals. The third is a technological change in the environment that creates heretofore undiscussed questions. It might involve mass transportation, air and water pollution, or air travel congestion. The fourth category is an actual imbalance, or bias, in the distribution of resources leading to such things as civil rights protest and union strikes.[4] A fifth type is ecological change, such as population explosion and black migration to Northern cities.

There are four types of external trigger mechanisms. The first is an act of war or military violence involving the United States as a direct combatant. Examples include the Vietnam war, the Pueblo seizure, and the dropping of atomic bombs on Hiroshima. The second category includes innovations in weapons technology involving such things as arms control, the Hotline between the Kremlin and the White House, and the deployment of an anti-ballistic system. The third type is an international conflict in which the United States is not a direct combatant, such as the conflicts in the Middle East and the Congo. The final category involves changing world alignment patterns that may affect American membership in the United Nations, troop commitments in the North Atlantic Treaty Organization, and the American role in the Organization of American States.

---

[4] Here the focus is on *actual* maldistribution of resources. A *perceived* maldistribution is covered by the "readjustor" type of issue initiator.

Issue Initiation and Trigger Mechanisms.   The formation of an issue is dependent on the dynamic interplay between the initiator and the trigger device. This can be seen in the following diagram:

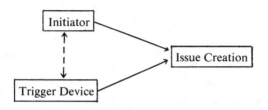

For example, a mine disaster itself does not create an issue. Many times in the past such an event has occurred with no ameliorative action. A link must be made between a grievance (or a triggering event) and an initiator who converts the problem into an issue for a private or a public reason.

In a system perspective, the inputs consist of the initiator and the event, or triggering mechanism, that transform the problem into an issue. The output is the agenda, which will be the focus of the next section. Transforming an issue into an agenda item will be the focus of succeeding chapters.

Agendas: What Are They?

In general terms, we have identified two basic types of political agendas. The first of these is the systemic agenda for political controversy. *The systemic agenda consists of all issues that are commonly perceived by members of the political community as meriting public attention and as involving matters within the legitimate jurisdiction of existing governmental authority.* Every local, state, and national political community will have a systemic agenda. The systemic agenda of the larger community may subsume items from the systemic agendas of subsidiary communities, but the two agendas will not necessarily correspond. For example, the systemic agenda of Boston may include items on the national agenda of controversy, such as pollution and crime in the streets, but will also include such items as the need for a new sports arena.

There are three prerequisites for an issue to obtain access to the systemic agenda: (1) widespread attention or at least awareness; (2) shared concern of a sizeable portion of the public that some type of action is required; and (3) a shared perception that the matter is an appropriate concern of some governmental unit and falls within the bounds of its authority. The terms "shared concern" and "shared perception" refer to the prevailing climate of opinion, which will be conditioned by the dominant norms, values, and ideology of a community. An issue requires the recognition of only a major portion of the polity, not the entire citizenry.

For an item or an issue to acquire public recognition, its supporters must have either access to the mass media or the resources necessary to reach people. They may require more than money and manpower; often the use of action rhetoric is essential. For example, use of terms such as *communist-inspired* or *anti-American* is a useful verbal ploy in attracting a larger audience than the original adherents of a cause.

In addition to gaining popular recognition, the issue must be perceived by a large number of people as both being subject to remedial action and requiring such action. In other words, action must be considered not only possible, but also necessary for the resolution of the issue. To foster such popular conviction, the mobilization of a significant number of groups or persons will normally be required.

Often, the fate of an issue in gaining systemic agenda status will hinge on whether or not it can be defined as being within the purview of legitimate governmental action. Perhaps one of the most devastating tactics that may be used to prevent an issue from reaching the systemic agenda is to deny that it falls within the bounds of governmental authority. For example, equal access to public accommodations was kept off the systemic agenda for some time because opponents successfully argued that the grievance fell outside the proper bounds of governmental authority.

The second type of agenda is the institutional, governmental, or formal agenda, which may be defined as *that set of items explicitly up for the active and serious consideration of authoritative decision-makers.* Therefore, any set of items up before any governmental body at the local, state, or national level will constitute an institutional agenda.

Two clarifications are in order regarding key terms in the above definition of a formal agenda. "Explicitly" refers to an issue involving action or policy alternatives or involving simply the identification of a problem requiring some action. An example of the former would be a proposal to raise the minimum wage to a specific level per hour. An illustration of the latter would be a reconsideration of certain restrictive loan practices of savings and loan institutions in the ghetto.

"Active and serious" are used to distinguish formal agenda items from what might be called "pseudo-agenda items." By pseudo-agenda, we mean any form of registering or acknowledging a demand without explicitly considering its merit. Decision-makers will often use such an agenda to assuage frustrations of constituency groups and to avoid political ramifications of a failure to acknowledge the demand. This typically occurs in a legislature where bills are placed in the hopper to placate some groups of activists with no real chance of action being taken.

Policy-makers will participate in the building of both systemic and institutional agendas. However, the natures of the two agendas are substantially different. The systemic agenda will be composed of fairly abstract and general items that do little more than identify a problem area. It will not necessarily suggest either the alternatives available or the means of coping with the problem. For example, it might include a vague item like "ending discrimination."

An institutional agenda will tend to be more specific, concrete, and limited in the number of items. It will identify, at least implicitly, those facets of a problem that are to be seriously considered by a decision-making body. An example would be a city council's consideration of alternative forms of local taxation for the support of public schools. It is possible for an item to get onto the formal agenda without having been a part of the systemic agenda. Each year, Congress considers many private bills of little social import or concern. However, it is unlikely that any issue involving substantial social consequences will gain standing on a governmental agenda unless it has first attained systemic agenda status.

CONTENT OF FORMAL AGENDAS. Formal agenda items can be divided into two major categories: *old items* and *new items*. *Old items* are those that have action alternatives delineated. They are predefined in most instances, except in specific cases (for example, the issue may not be whether workers will receive a 5 percent or a 10 percent raise, but whether they will get a raise at all).

There are two agenda components under the general heading of *old items*. Habitual items include those that come up for regular review. Examples would be budget items such as personnel pay and fights between existing agencies for a larger slice of the federal budget.

Recurrent items are those that occur with some periodicity, but need not appear at regular intervals. Examples would include governmental reorganization and regulation arising from a concern for efficiency or economy or both, rules changes in the legislature (for example, the filibuster in the Senate), Congressional reform, tariff items, tax reform, and social security increases or extensions.

The second general heading, *new items,* refers to those components that have no predetermined definitions, but are flexible in their interpretation or development. The first subdivision would include automatic or spontaneous issues appearing as an action or reaction of a key decision-maker in a specific situation. Examples include public employee or major industry strikes with a substantial impact on the economy or our military strength, the steel crisis under President Truman during the Korean War, foreign policy crises (e.g., Korea, Cuba, and the Dominican Republic), and innovations in foreign policy (e.g., American entrance into the United Nations, the test ban treaty, and the nuclear proliferation treaty).

A second component of *new items* is channeled items, those issues channeled to the agenda by the mobilization of mass support or by the activation of significant public groups (e.g., unions). Examples of issues with mass support include the civil rights issues of the 1960's and the gun control issue. Illustrations of issues backed by significant public groups include the Taft-Hartley repeal effort and the farm parity program.

An issue need not be static or confined to one category throughout its existence. At any point in time, it may be redefined. An example of a dynamic issue is the Vietnam policy. Initially, it became a spontaneous issue when President Eisenhower committed several hundred advisers in the late 1950's. The issue of expanded commitment became recurrent under Presidents Kennedy and Johnson. By 1963, the dispute appeared on the docket with great regularity. It continued in this form until opposition to the war—a channelized item begun by peace groups—raised the question of the legitimacy of American involvement. The peace groups expanded concern with American involvement until it became the policy stance of a major presidential candidate in 1968.

THE FORM OF AN INSTITUTIONAL AGENDA.   The explicit form of the formal agenda may be found in the calendar of authoritative decision-making bodies such as legislatures, high courts, or regulatory agencies.[5] Unless an item appears on some docket, it will not be considered to be an agenda item. Agenda composition will vary over time. However, recurrent or habitual items will be the most numerous. They tend to receive priority from the decision-makers, who constantly find that their time is limited and that their agenda is overloaded. Spontaneous, or automatic, items take precedence over channeled items, so it is very difficult to get new issues on the agenda. Decision-makers presume that older problems warrant more attention because of their longevity and the greater familiarity officials have with them.

Differential Access to Institutional Gatekeepers

The content of a formal agenda will tend to reflect structural and institutional biases found within the system. These biases arise from differential resources among individuals and groups and concomitant differences in access. For an issue to attain agenda status, it must command the support of at least some key decision-makers, for they are the ultimate guardians of the formal agenda.

Political leaders are active participants in the agenda-building process, not simply impartial arbiters of issue disputes. As Bauer, Pool, and Dexter note:

> Congress is not a passive body, registering already-existent public views forced on its attention by public pressures. Congress,

[5] Calendars normally provide predefined agendas for both the legislature and the court. However, most legislatures have some procedure to allow items to be entered on the agenda at the request of one decision-maker without going through the normal procedures of agenda specification. For example, in the Congress, this procedure involves the private calendar. That calendar will be excluded from our analysis, which focuses on the public and union calendars, where most issues of public import will be found.

second only to the president, is, rather the major institution for initiating and creating political issues and projecting them into a national civic debate.[6]

The strategic location of these leaders assures them of media visibility when they want to promote an issue and places them in an excellent position to bargain with other decision-makers over formal agenda content. Because they have fairly direct control over what will appear on the formal agenda and considerable freedom to choose among the plethora of issues competing for attention, they can insist that an issue of concern to them be considered in return for agreement to consider an issue that is salient to another decision-maker or set of decision-makers.

It is easy then to understand why access to one or more key officials is so important to political groups. As one commentator noted,

> The development and improvement of such access is a common denominator of the tactics of all of them, frequently leading to efforts to exclude competing groups from equivalent access or to set up new decision points access to which can be monopolized by a particular group.[7]

Some groups have a greater ease of access than others, and are thus more likely to get their demands placed on an agenda.

This differential responsiveness arises from a variety of factors. First, the decision-maker may be indebted to a particular group or identify himself as a member of that group. Second, some groups have more resources than others or are better able to mobilize their resources. Third, some groups are located so strategically in the social or economic structure of society that their interests cannot be ignored (for example, big business and agriculture). Fourth, some groups (such as doctors, lawyers and church leaders) are held in greater esteem by the public than others and thus can command greater access to decision-makers. As a consequence, certain groups are more likely than others to receive attention from decision-makers when they come up with new demands. Farmers have an inherent advantage over many other groups in obtaining action on their needs

[6] Raymond Bauer, Ithiel Pool and Lewis Dexter, *American Business and Public Policy* (New York: Atherton Press, 1963), p. 478.
[7] David Truman, *The Governmental Process* (New York: Knopf, 1964), p. 264.

because there are many decision-makers who identify themselves with farm groups and because agriculture occupies a pivotal position in the American economy.

A group may encounter different types of responses from different levels or branches of the government. When the National Association for the Advancement of Colored People first started to press its demands, it focused on the Congress and the presidency, but received no support. However, the group was much more effective when it focused on a judicial strategy of making gains in civil rights through a series of court cases. Thus, differential responsiveness may result from the type of governmental unit petitioned as well as from differences among groups themselves.

Political parties also play an important part in translating issues into agenda items.[8] To assure support, they will often seek out and identify themselves with issues that are salient to large portions of the populace. Typically, these issues are identified in the party platform in general terms and with considerable ambiguity. However, as Truman notes:

> The significance of preparing a platform lies primarily in the evidence that the negotiations provide concerning what groups will have access to the developing national party organization. . . . Interest group leaders are aware that the real settlement of the issues they are concerned with . . . will take place later; in the platform, they seek tentative assurance of a voice in that settlement. To maximize this assurance, political interest groups normally seek recognition in the platforms of both major parties.[9]

Certainly recognition on a party platform is at least indicative of an issue attaining standing on the systemic agenda of political controversy.[10]

The media can also play a very important role in elevating issues to the systemic agenda and increasing their chances of receiving

[8] See, for example, Everett C. Ladd, Jr., *American Political Parties* (New York: W. W. Norton and Company, 1970).

[9] Truman, *op. cit.,* p. 285.

[10] Significant differences in the platforms of the two major parties may portend a major alteration in the national systemic agenda. This change may be realized through what Key called "a critical election." Certainly a critical, or realigning, election may be taken as an indicator of a major shift in the systemic agenda. See V. O. Key, *Politics, Parties and Pressure Groups.* 5th ed. (New York: Thomas Crowell Company, 1964), pp. 520–36.

formal agenda consideration. Certain personages in the media can act as opinion leaders in bringing publicity to a particular issue. Examples of individuals who have gained a larger audience for a dispute include Walter Lippmann, Jack Anderson, and Drew Pearson. Individuals who have acquired an audience simply by constantly appearing in the news can also publicize an issue. Ralph Nader has a ready-made constituency stemming from his many attacks on various inefficient and unscrupulous business practices.

Differential Legitimacy

While most observers grant that there are inequalities in access to decision-makers, they argue that the existence of multiple points of access owing to different levels and branches of government has the net effect of insuring widespread contacts. Further, the existence of dispersed inequalities (that is, the fact that groups having great resources in one area may not have comparable resources in other areas) supposedly assures that no group will be without political influence in some areas. However, this argument fails to consider the relatively stable pattern of differential legitimacy accorded various social groupings. Differences in accessibility to decision-makers are a function of the relative legitimacy of various groups. For example, a proposal advanced by a group of businessmen to improve traffic flows into the downtown business area is more likely to receive the attention of decision-makers than a counterproposal by ghetto residents to develop more extensive and effective mass transit systems.

The problem confronted by any newly formed group is often how to legitimize the group and the interest represented rather than how to legitimize a particular issue position. The legitimacy of the group will be greatly enhanced by the status and community standing of its members. In other words, people without resources (for example, lower-income groups) will have greater difficulty attaining legitimacy than their higher-income counterparts. For example, the anti-war movement initially promoted by student groups who traditionally have little political standing received little public support until more socially prominent persons and groups entered the fray on their behalf (for example, business groups, military leaders, clergymen, and senators).

Systemic Constraints on Agenda Entrance

Even if an issue is promoted by a group that is perceived to be legitimate, its appearance on a formal agenda may be problematic owing to cultural constraints on the range of issues that are considered legitimate topics for governmental action. Any institutional agenda will be restricted by the prevailing popular sentiment as to what constitutes appropriate matters for governmental attention. For example, federal aid to education was long considered by many to be an inappropriate area for federal governmental action, a fact that precluded active and serious consideration of the merits of the issue for decades. Legitimizing issues that are considered outside of the governmental realm is difficult and normally takes a long time. The net effect of this is that new demands of particularly disadvantaged or deprived groups are the least likely to receive attention on either the systemic agenda of controversy or the institutional agenda.

6

Issue Characteristics
and Relevant Publics

This chapter focuses on the characteristics of issues that bear on whether or not the issues are likely to reach a public docket. In addition, issue expansion is reconsidered in relation to various groups within the populace to whom the initial disputants can effectively plead for additional support.

Types of Issues

Theodore Lowi has asserted that there are three major types of policies, or types of issues that may be placed on the docket: distribution, regulation, and redistribution. The types are mutually exclusive, and every policy can be encapsulated under one. Lowi asserts that all of these policy areas are distinct in that they "constitute real arenas of power. Each arena tends to develop its own characteristic political structure, political process, elites, and group relations." [1]

Distributive policy involves short run considerations to which a government must give priority. Within this domain are "pork barrel"

[1] Theodore Lowi, "American Business, Public Policy, Case Studies and Political Theory," World Politics 16 (1964), pp. 689–90.

issues such as rivers and harbors, defense authorizations, services for the business and labor constituencies, and other patronage issues. These issues are an accumulation of a number of fragmented, piecemeal policies. The achievement of such policies usually involves legislative coalitions and log-rolling.

As for their implications for conflict, there is no aggregation of disputes, because issues are resolved in a piecemeal fashion. Decisions are made, but few people, even bureaucrats, are completely aware of what the issues involve. Such issues are resolved outside of the public arena with little likelihood that they will be expanded to involve subgroups within the populace.

Regulatory policies resemble distributive policies, for they are also specific and individual in effect. They include questions involving labor-management relations and questions of administrative decree. While decisions are made on an individual level, they can be aggregated to indicate an overall policy direction.

In regulatory policies, administrators are unable to resolve the conflicts, which means the issues revert to Congress, where such disputes are resolved. In this instance, Lowi observes, "Congress and the 'balance of power' seem to play the classic role attributed to them by the pluralists." [2] Lowi argues that his scheme is dynamic and that an issue can move from category to category. He asserts, for example, that tariff legislation is moving from the distributive to the regulatory arena. For that reason, the pressure group is not the complete answer to how the issue gained access to a formal agenda.

The third type of policy involves redistribution. The basis of differentiation is that redistributive issues usually involve large numbers of people, more than either of the previous categories. These issues, including such matters as the income tax and various welfare state programs, tend to be defined along class lines. Redistributive issues are usually more likely to attain formal agenda standing than other types of issues because of the economic cleavage. Issues that involve "haves versus the havenots" are more likely to gain quick access to the docket because large numbers of people are involved. As Lowi observes:

> They [redistributive issues] cut closer than any others . . . in what are roughly class terms. If there is ever any cohesion within the

[2] *Ibid.,* p. 699.

peak associations [e.g., social class], it occurs on redistributive issues, and their rhetoric suggests that they occupy themselves most
of the time with these.[3]

For example, Lowi found that the Connecticut chapter of the
Manufacturers' Association has published more statements over a ten-
year period on redistributive issues (e.g., general labor relations and
wages) than on regulative matters (e.g., trade practices, anti-trust,
fair trade, and basing points). As Lowi asserts in the language of
agenda-building, "They [associations] gain identity to the extent that
they can define the issue in redistributive terms." [4]

While Lowi attempts to identify the basic typology of issues,
which may explain the subsequent levels of conflict, his scheme has
certain limitations. Because his formulations rely on substantive
rather than analytic criteria, he has at best nominal categories for
characterizing issues. Thus, while he asserts that his scheme is dynamic, change can occur only in a categorical sense. He provides us
with no incremental gradations. Moreover, by asserting that his
scheme is dynamic, he obscures the clarity that it might otherwise
have. His categories, as a result, become diffuse, and distinctions become unclear. Further, his classifications seem to be applicable only
to domestic issues and certainly do not provide dimensions along
which any and all issues might be differentiated. What is needed is a
scheme that allows any issue to be characterized in terms of certain
fundamental dimensions that will bear on the prospects of that issue
gaining access to the political agenda.

Issue Characteristics

The key may be found by focusing not on the content of issues but
rather on the nature of conflict itself. The issues in a conflict will
vary along several dimensions. How an issue is defined, explicitly or
implicitly, will have important bearing on the nature and eventual
outcome of a conflict. The five fundamental definitional dimensions
include (1) the degree of specificity, (2) the scope of social significance, (3) the extent of temporal relevance, (4) the degree of com-

[3] *Ibid.,* p. 707.
[4] *Ibid.,* p. 711.

plexity, and (5) the degree of categorical precedence.[5] Each of these dimensions describes a continuum along which an issue must be defined.[6]

Specificity refers to how abstractly or concretely an issue will be defined.[7] There is a tremendous difference between a group that attempts to remove "obscene literature" from local bookstores and a similar group in another city that defines the issue as a list of specific items that should be impounded by the local police department. Measures of specificity include the extent to which specific objectives are enunciated, the number of condensation symbols that are used as opposed to the number of referential symbols in a statement of group objectives, and the perception of the disputants as to the concreteness of the issue struggle.

The second dimension, *social significance,* relates to whether an issue is peculiar to the immediate disputants or has more general significance.[8] Social significance is similar to what Kenneth Gergen calls "impact." "One can speak of issue impact to refer to the number of persons who will potentially be affected. . . . The greater the impact, the more people who will be seeking active engagement in the decision-making process." [9] For example, an issue dealing with how

[5] Though we would not contend that we have achieved logical closure, we would contend that these are the major definitional dimensions. They are drawn from various sources, but the reader will note their similarity to Talcott Parson's pattern variables. See Parsons and Edward Shils (eds.), *Toward A General Theory of Action* (New York: Harper, 1951), pp. 76–91.

[6] There are alternative ways of conceptualizing how different issues are categorized and diffused to various publics. For example, Everett Rogers stipulated five characteristics that affect the rate of adoption of an innovation: (1) relative advantage, the extent to which it is superior to competing items; (2) compatibility, the extent to which the innovation is aligned with key values; (3) complexity, the extent to which it can be used with ease; (4) divisibility, the likelihood that it can be diffused on a limited basis; and (5) communicability, or the extent to which results of an innovation can be channeled to others. See Rogers, *The Diffusion of Innovation* (New York: Free Press, 1962), p. 146. For an alternate approach which specifies pre-decisional facets such as scope, perception, intensity, definition and issue content, see Charles O. Jones, *An Introduction to Public Policy* (Belmont, Calif.: Wadsworth Publishing Company, 1970), pp. 32–42.

[7] Cf. Murray Edelman, *The Symbolic Uses of Politics* (Urbana: University of Illinois Press, 1964).

[8] Parsons and Shils, *op. cit.,* pp. 76–84.

[9] Kenneth Gergen, "Assessing the Leverage Points in the Process of Policy Formation," in Raymond Bauer and Kenneth Gergen (eds.), *The Study of Policy Formation* (New York: Free Press, 1968), p. 193.

much poultry farmers are going to receive in governmental subsidy each month would be considered less socially significant than the anti-poverty campaign of the national government. A dispute over the impact of a particular chemical in polluting bodies of water throughout the nation would be more significant than a ruling by the Interstate Commerce Commission on the maximum number of pounds that can be carried by vehicles in interstate commerce. Examples of the possible measures of social significance are the amount of money involved in the potential program and the number of people affected if the program goes into operation with either an objective or a perceptual measure.

The third continuum, *temporal relevance,* denotes the extent to which an issue has short range, circumstantial relevance or more enduring, fundamental relevance.[10] Issues that are going to have implications above and beyond the resolution of the particular issue at one point in time and one level in government are temporally relevant.

For example, the issue of student militancy concerns immediate specific grievances, such as the creation of a black studies program and the admission of more black students. But more basic than this is the questioning of the whole authority structure within the university, including the relationship between trustees, bureaucrats, faculty, and students. In addition, the role of the university vis-a-vis the government is going through a reappraisal, with secret research and war-based projects sponsored by public agencies coming under criticism. Such questions are going to become more important with the passage of time once black students are enrolled in greater numbers and the immediate grievances are forgotten. Thus, such an issue has long run implications for the entire university environment even though it may be couched in short run objectives.

Examples of likely measures of this dimension might include perceptions of time necessary to implement a desired program by both the disputants and the relevant governmental officials, and an evaluation by the disputants and bureaucrats of what the real issue is in a particular conflict.

Complexity, our fourth dimension, concerns how an issue will be delineated along a continuum from the highly complex and techni-

---

[10] Cf. Herbert Spiro, "Comparative Politics: A Comprehensive Approach," *American Political Science Review* 56 (1962), p. 577.

cal to the simple and easily understood.[11] On this continuum, the passage of a higher minimum wage for specific groups would be a fairly simplistic issue. A more technical dispute would involve the conservationist groups who are attempting to limit the use of insect sprays. This issue has been placed in the hands of two groups of competing scientists, representing naturalists and chemical companies, who utilize terminology that is beyond the grasp of the layman.

A more familiar example of a complex issue would be the fight over the desirability of a particular weapons system. The employment of an anti-missile system, for example, even that part of the system that is not shrouded in national secrecy, is highly complex and understandable to very few individuals, even scientists. Expertise can be crucial if used to define issues in a tone beneficial to one side. As Lewis Dexter has written: "Military men often belong to a category of technological specialists . . . who can to a considerable degree get their own way by posing the questions for the legislature." [12]

Complexity is often a matter of perception and is not necessarily related to the number of facets of the issue. Often complex issues can be defined as relatively simple issues if the disputants believe they have a personal stake in their resolution. For example, consider the following case posed by Dexter:

> Even more basic . . . is the little word technical. Congressmen tend to regard as "technical" such questions for "professional" military men as the nature of war plans. But they regard as "non-technical" . . . such matters as the way oil is stored in overseas installations or how service credit shall be allocated for ROTC . . . problems of the type which at some universities would be thankfully left as a "technical matter" for registrars to decide.[13]

Thus, it is relevant for the study of agenda-building to consider the extent to which technicalizing the issue will remove or involve the decision-makers, and on what issues "professional and technical matters should be left to professional and technical men." [14]

---

[11] David Truman, *The Governmental Process* (New York: Knopf, 1951), p. 361. Also see Edelman, *op. cit.*, pp. 134–48.
[12] Lewis Dexter, "Congressmen and the Making of Military Policy," in Robert Peabody and Nelson Polsby (eds.), *New Perspectives on the House of Representatives* (Chicago: Rand McNally, 1963), 314–15.
[13] *Ibid.*, p. 321.
[14] *Ibid.*, p. 323.

Examples of the possible measures of complexity include the number of people required to administer a program should it be placed on the formal agenda and enacted into law, the number of levels of government involved or the number of governmental departments concerned, and the extent to which the issues are really understood by the participants. Another measure might be an estimate of the number of people with advanced degrees who are taking an active part in the dispute. On fairly complex issues, the interested subgroups will tend to have very little knowledge of what is actually involved other than a broad policy preference.

Our fifth dimension, *categorical precedence,* indicates the extent to which an issue is a routine matter having more or less clear precedents (and consequently probable procedures for its resolution) or, conversely, the extent to which it is extraordinary.[15] For example, an issue with a great deal of precedence would be the government's resolution of major contract disputes between labor and management. The procedure is standardized to the extent that it resembles a ritual with an offer and counter-offer, threat and counter-threat, and ultimate government mediation or arbitration often after a costly work layoff.

The extent of categorical precedence is a very important factor in determining how disputes will be resolved. Roger Fisher suggests that it is a stabilizing influence: "Recognizing where possible that a dispute involves a question of the application of principle rather than the central principle itself should make it possible to decrease the stakes." [16] Gamson asserts that the extent to which such processes have been clearly delineated in the past is a key to how conflict will be resolved. He writes:

> By de-emphasizing the precedent setting aspects of decisions and by emphasizing their ad hoc nature, by deciding issues in bits and pieces rather than taking them in omnibus form, authorities can reduce the tendency for their decisions to lead to attitudes of confidence or alienation. . . . A partisan group may wish to emphasize the symbolic aspects of an issue and be adverse to having decisions

[15] Robert Dubin, "Industrial Conflict and Social Welfare," *Journal of Conflict Resolution* 1 (1957), p. 187.
[16] Roger Fisher, "Fractionating Conflict," in Roger Fisher (ed.), *International Conflict and Behavioral Science* (New York: Basic Books, 1964), p. 100.

made in such a way that no new principle or precedent is established.[17]

An example of an issue dispute whose guidelines were not clear involves university protesters. The takeover of buildings at Columbia and other institutions left college officials unclear as to what action to take. In the Columbia case, there were no clear guidelines other than a university aversion to using outside force (ie., New York City police), and officials tended to establish new norms as they attempted to grapple with the intricacies of the problem.

Often one side will treat an issue conventionally, according to set guidelines, while the other side may want it to be treated as unique without a consideration of precedents. This is a major point of the cleavage between people involved in the drug debate. Those advocating stringent penalties want offenders treated as common criminals. Others stress medical treatment and placement in a medical facility rather than imprisonment.

Types of indicators that might be used to measure precedence include the number of similar issues in the past (at the local, state, and national level) and the degree of success in implementation, the frequency of such programs implemented in the past, and perceptual knowledge of such precedents by the disputants and relevant or affected decision-makers. The last example might include knowledge of prior programs that were not actually precedents for the dispute at hand, but were believed to be pace setters.

The contending parties will play an active role in defining issues along some or all of these dimensions. Regardless of emphasis, however, all issues can be evaluated in terms of the above criteria. The important point is that issue definition is by no means an *a priori* given. The conflicting parties will not necessarily agree on how the issues are to be defined. As Schattschneider has commented:

> Political conflict is not like an intercollegiate debate in which the opponents agree in advance on a definition of the issues. As a matter of fact, the definition of the alternatives is the supreme instrument of power.[18]

[17] William Gamson, *Power and Discontent* (Homewood, Ill.: Dorsey Press, 1968), 52.
[18] E. E. Schattschneider, *The Semi-Sovereign People* (New York: Holt, 1960), p. 68.

Thus, conflicts over issues can change over time. For example, a pro-fluoridation group, frustrated in its attempt to reach the formal agenda in a local community in one year, might switch its strategy to make the issue more attractive, focusing on a more emotional appeal with a public education campaign. In this way, formal agenda status is achieved via standing on the systemic agenda of public controversy. Issues can also change within the context of the same attempt. A group might spend a month trying to gain the governmental agenda, become frustrated, drop the campaign, and switch to a completely different strategy.

Although the focus of this work is not what happens after the issue gains institutional agenda status, one further clarification is necessary. Decision-makers do not necessarily reflect the pre-decisional bias in confronting an issue. For example, when a group with overwhelming support in a community succeeds in getting the attention of the elected leaders, the decision-makers will not necessarily take action supporting that group's stance. They may do something at odds with the issue stance of the group, or they may co-opt the issue for themselves.

Control over how the issues of conflict are defined means control over the choice of battlefields upon which a conflict will take place. A group will always select a battlefield that gives it an advantage in terms of potential support.

Contending Parties

Before carrying our discussion of issue conflict further, we must consider the nature of the conflicting parties. It will be recalled that we are interested strictly in group conflicts. What we want to consider are the characteristics of groups that will have bearing on a conflict. For the sake of brevity, we will not dwell in detail upon specific characteristics. Rather, we will consider them collectively in terms of organizational scale. This is a summary variable referring to such things as organizational skills, extensity and intensity of communications, size, and resources.[19]

The scale of the groups involved in a controversy is of vital im-

[19] Cf. Scott Greer, *The Emerging City* (New York: Free Press, 1962), passim.

portance in that it indicates the number of persons immediately affected by the conflict and measures the relative strength of the contending camps. Further, the scale of the disputants will be an important determinant of the general visibility of a conflict and the consequent probability of its expansion.

Relevant Publics

For various groupings to become aware of the development of a particular issue, the issue must be relevant or salient. An issue will become "relevant" to a public to the extent to which it is defined as "salient" to the members of a particular group. Salience is the sum response of the audience to the five aforementioned characteristics and how they are interwoven during the course of a controversy. Contending groups attempt to define the five characteristics in terms of salience for onlookers. As Bauer has written:

> In order to understand or predict the way in which a given issue will be handled, we must determine the salience which the issue has relative to other things with which the individual has to cope. And this is seldom self-evident. The salience of an issue can be considered in a temporal sense in that, at a given moment in time, a person has a limitation on the resources, including time, he can muster.[20]

What Bauer has called "salience," Gergen has identified as "relevance," but both refer to the way in which a person becomes sensitized to an issue. Gergen stresses that the individual must be able to translate the issue into one that will have direct impact on his life.

> People vary greatly in their relationship to a given public issue and different issues may impinge on a person in varying degrees. . . . One can thus speak of the relevance of a given issue for a given person and compare the relevance of a single issue for different people. . . . An issue will be relevant to an individual to the extent that for him it can potentially modify the status quo. . . . The

[20] Raymond Bauer, "The Policy Process," in Raymond Bauer and Kenneth Gergen (eds.), *The Study of Policy Formation* (New York: Free Press, 1968), 17.

greater the relevance of an issue to a person, the stronger will be his attempt to exert leverage.[21]

Delineation of Various Publics

So far we have largely restricted our primary focus to direct participants in a conflict; however, we know that social conflicts do not occur in a vacuum. According to Schattschneider:

> Every fight consists of two parts: (1) a few individuals who are actively engaged at the center and (2) the audience that is irresistibly attracted to the scene. The latter are an integral part of the overall situation.[22]

Turning our attention now to the audience, or spectators of a conflict (persons who may subsequently be drawn into the conflict), we may distinguish several components.

Over four decades ago, John Dewey pointed out the rather simple fact that some human actions have consequences for others who are not immediate participants in the action.[23] The "others" who perceive these consequences constitute the audience of a conflict, or what Dewey calls its "public." A rather important implication that follows from this is that there is not a single, undifferentiated public; a public is "always specific to a particular situation or issue." [24] The structure of the public and the level of public concern with respect to any conflict will be functions of the nature of that conflict. Society, then, at any point in time will be composed of an overlapping complex of specific and general publics that may or may not become relevant in a given dispute.

Thus, the public is defined by the subject matter at hand and is subject to change in its composition. Dewey assumed that decisions reflect the interest of the public, situationally defined. The principal

[21] Kenneth Gergen, "Assessing the Leverage Points in the Process of Policy Formation," in *Ibid.*, pp. 183–84.
[22] Schattschneider, *op. cit.*, p. 1.
[23] John Dewey, *The Public and Its Problems* (New York: Holt, 1927), pp. 12–17.
[24] Truman, *op. cit.*, p. 219.

problem is one of identifying relevant boundaries for different sub-groups within the population.[25]

Others have addressed the problem of stipulating various publics that are relevant in different types of issue contexts. Norton Long argues that community conflict is continuous, involving a variety of overlapping groups that can become relevant in different types of dynamic conflict situations. According to Long:

> Individuals may play a number of games. . . . Transfer from one game [i.e., conflict] to another is, of course, possible, and the simultaneous playing of roles in two or more games is an important manner of linking separate games. Sharing a common territorial field, . . . the players in one game make use of the players in another and are, in turn made use of by them. . . . Each is a piece in the chess game of the other . . . with a different end in view.[26]

In an analysis of civil rights conflict, Danzger found important differences between integrationists and segregationists in terms of their related publics (that is, the people who are affiliated with them).

> Different players are involved in the different issues. One should also note that it is not simply that they are involved, but that their involvement brings to bear their resources. One major power resource is the organization of the groups themselves. [In the civil rights study], segregations [placed] . . . increasing reliance on organizations between 1958 and 1962.[27]

Since issue conflicts are played out in front of an audience, it is useful to identify four general types of publics. They range from the most involved to the general populace.

SPECIFIC PUBLICS: IDENTIFICATION GROUPS.   The "public of a group may be thought of as an aggregate of individuals who are aware, or who can be made aware, of various possible consequences of the group's action. . . ."[28] As conceived here, more specifically,

[25] Dewey, *op. cit.*, pp. 12–17.
[26] Norton Long, "The Local Community as an Ecology of Games," *American Journal of Sociology* 44 (1958), p. 253.
[27] Herbert Danzger, "A Quantified Description of Community Conflict," *American Behavioral Scientist* 12 (1968), p. 12.
[28] Truman, *op. cit.*, p. 218.

the public of a given group refers to those groups who are oriented towards, or focus attention upon, that group, identifying their interests generally with those of that group or having a persistent sympathy with its generic interests.

The public of a group will consist of the members of a non-involved synthetic grouping that may be called an *identification group*.[29] The ties between the members of an identification group will vary in strength, but will, nonetheless, tend to be relatively stable and lasting. The members of such a grouping will tend to be the most sensitive segment of the general population should conflicts involving any of its member-groups arise. They will be the first segment of the audience to become involved in a conflict should it expand beyond those initially involved in a dispute.

SPECIFIC PUBLICS: ATTENTION GROUPS.   In addition to the publics of the groups immediately involved, we may distinguish at least analytically what might be called issue publics, which correspond to what Rosenau has labeled *attention groups*.[30] Persons in such groups are disinterested in most issues, but they are informed about and interested in certain specific issues. In fact, once an issue is raised in their sphere of concern, they become readily mobilizable. Thus, attention groups are one of the first segments of the audience to enter an expanding conflict. Like identification groups, they will be aware of a dispute long before it becomes visible or at least before it concerns the general public. However, attention group participation will tend to be dependent on the issues involved in a conflict, whereas identification group involvement centers on the group affiliations of the combatants.[31]

Attention groups include pressure groups with an interest in an issue or a set of issues. For example, when the Reverend Jessie Gray

[29] Cf. V. O. Key, *Public Opinion and American Democracy* (New York: Knopf, 1961), p. 220.
[30] James Rosenau, *Public Opinion and Foreign Policy* (New York: Random House, 1961), p. 37.
[31] This resembles what Charles Jones has called a "policy constituency." When a legislator is suffering from severe role strain, "then he will rely on his perception of the interests affected (his 'policy constituency')." See Charles Jones, "Representation in Congress: The Case of the House Agriculture Committee," *American Political Science Review* 55 (1961), p. 367.

led the Harlem rent strike of 1968, he had the support of a number of attention groups, including New York City civil rights groups.[32]

MASS PUBLICS: ATTENTIVE PUBLIC. Turning from specific publics to the general population, we may identify what Almond has called the *attentive public*,[33] a generally informed and interested stratum of the population. Though not homogeneous, the attentive public tends to be relatively stable in composition and comes disproportionately from the more educated and higher income groups.[34] It is from this stratum that the opinion leaders identified by Elihu Katz and Paul Lazarsfeld come.[35] It is largely through these persons that less active and less interested segments of the population become aware of a conflict.

There is some indication that the size of the attentive public is increasing as the general educational level of the population increases. Estimates of its size vary, but normally not more than 10 percent of the public is included.[36] As Rosenau asserts:

> The attentive public consists . . . of a permanent core of multi-issue members and a number of single-issue persons whose identity is constantly changing as the rise of new issues and the attenuation of old ones activate and dissolve corresponding attention groups. . . . [They] are the multi-issue citizens who have a broad-gauged and consistent concern about public affairs.[37]

MASS PUBLICS: GENERAL PUBLIC. Finally, and again following Almond, we may speak of a *general public*,[38] that part of the population that is less active, less interested, and less informed. It is the last segment of the audience to become involved in a conflict. For the general public to be activated, the issues must be highly generalized

---

[32] For a review of the Harlem rent strike, see Michael Lipsky, "Rent Strikes: Poor Man's Weapon," *Transaction* 6 No. 4 (February, 1969), pp. 10–15.

[33] Gabriel Almond, *The American People and Foreign Policy* (New York: Harcourt, 1950), p. 138.

[34] Rosenau, *op. cit.*, p. 39.

[35] Elihu Katz and Paul Lazarsfeld, *Personal Influence* (Glencoe: Free Press, 1955).

[36] James Rosenau, *The Attentive Public and Foreign Policy: A Theory of Growth and Some New Evidence* (Princeton: Center of International Studies, 1968), pp. 2–5, 22–48.

[37] *Ibid.*, p. 20.

[38] Almond, *op. cit.*, p. 138.

and symbolic. In fact, it is highly unlikely that this portion of the population will ever be mobilized by a given conflict.[39] However, it must be kept in mind that while the general public "is characterized by a sense of identification and reacts to general stimuli, it also contains a variety of interests and groups which are affected differentially by both general and specific stimuli." [40] The general public for a given situation or set of issues may include specific publics for other situations and issues.

In discussing the general public, we are dealing with a statistical artifact, since the entire public is not likely to be activated by any specific issue. It is unusual for a large segment of the populace to become involved. The general public will not necessarily be responsive to, or even aware of, an issue that received sustained media attention. For example, the decision to appoint Abe Fortas to the position of Chief Justice received a lot of publicity during the summer of 1968, yet most people were unaware of the issue.

When the populace does become interested in an issue, its concern will be ephemeral and its response unorganized. After Martin Luther King and Senator Robert Kennedy were assassinated, there was a great outpouring of grief which was channeled into a call for stronger laws concerning the use of firearms. Decision-makers were swamped with letters urging stronger laws, but the mass response was not strategically directed. Letters were sent to Senator Edward Kennedy, who was not active in that legislative matter at the time, and to other senators who were already publicly committed to an issue position. Solicitations were not concentrated on key members of pivotal committees concerned with gun control. Within a month, the hurrah died down and public pressure for legislation relapsed to the same stratum of the populace that had been active in the past.

A Specific Example of Conflict Expansion

The New York City teacher's strike illustrates a conflict that expanded to include identification groups, attention groups, the attentive public, and the general public. The conflict began as a dispute

[39] Key, *op. cit.*, p. 284.
[40] *Ibid.*

between a group of teachers and a local school board. The teacher's union (an identification group) immediately rallied to the support of the teachers, calling their dismissal an issue on which all teachers must take a stand. Other municipal unions (additional identification groups) rallied behind the teacher's union, since all workers had a stake in the dispute. As the conflict expanded and was redefined, the issue of anti-Semitism was raised. This brought the Jewish residents of New York City (an attention group) into the fray. They sided with the teachers only because of the larger issues involved. Of course, by this time the better informed strata of the general public had become aware of the conflict, which eventually filtered to the general public when the teachers went on strike.

7

The Dynamics of Issue Expansion

We have attempted to develop a typology of key issue characteristics and to identify different groupings within the general public. Now we must consider the relationship between types of issues and the sort of support they will attract. The underlying proposition is that the greater the size of the audience to which an issue can be enlarged, the greater the likelihood that it will attain systemic agenda standing and thus access to a formal agenda. That is not to say that all issues must be expanded to the mass public to make the docket, but simply that there is an increased probability of success if the conflict is visible to a large number of people.

The following diagram shows the relationship between issue characteristics and issue expansion:

Before specifying the set of relationships, a few clarifying notes are in order. The four publics outlined in the last chapter may be viewed as four concentric circles, each including more people than the preceding one. When we discuss expansion to a larger public, we mean from the identification group to an attention group and eventually to the more general public. Issues that have characteristic X are likely to be recognized by more people than issues that do not have it.[1]

A public can be involved in an issue without taking part in an action such as picketing, writing letters to decision-makers, or contributing money to a campaign. Such activities are likely to be limited to identification groups regardless of the issue and how many are involved from other publics. We consider an issue to be expanded to a "public" when people within that public are aware that the issue is contested and are positively or negatively attracted to it. Only a sizable section of the mass public need be aware of an issue to expand it to that level, because all of the mass will never be involved. Measures of awareness would include public opinion polls in which people are queried about their knowledge of public issues. Since an issue is not static, and since groups may lose interest as a conflict proceeds, our propositions refer only to the gaining of exposure for a conflict or the reacquiring of concern for the outcome if interest is lost.[2] *Awareness,* when used in reference to issue expansion, does not imply a detailed knowledge of an issue. That type of knowledge is usually possessed only by identification groups.[3]

[1] Further, when the set of propositions is delineated, we do not make the assumption that the issue conflict is static. Issues can change from characteristic X to non-X during the course of a controversy. The variables are assumed to be continuous. When we speak of an issue being "ambiguous" or "concrete," we mean in a relative sense; there are elements of both in all issues.

[2] For example, one author suggested that there are three aspects in researching public awareness: " (1) information concerning key issues . . . (2) information concerning other individuals involved in the issue area [and] . . . (3) ratings of all [persons] on relevant policy phase[s]." See Kenneth Gergen, "Assessing the Leverage Points in the Process of Policy Formation," in Raymond Bauer and Kenneth Gergen (eds.), *The Study of Policy Formation* (New York: Free Press, 1968), p. 199.

[3] Our focus is on how issues become defined as the key element in determining whether they will be expanded. This is not to say that "resources" such as publicity, financing, and number of people initially involved will not be important. However, our emphasis will be on the nature of the issue and the symbols as they relate to enlargement. Other literature has adequately covered the resource phase. For example, see *Ibid.,* pp. 185–89.

Propositions Linking Issue Characteristics
and Issue Expansion

CONCRETENESS.   Issues are likely to be expanded to a larger public if they can be defined broadly to appeal to more subgroups within the populace. *The more ambiguously an issue is defined, the greater the likelihood that it will reach an expanded public.*[4]

A dispute between the truckers and the railroads in Pennsylvania illustrates this proposition. Initially, in the early 1950's, the conflict concerned the number of pounds that constitutes a maximum load for a truck engaged in long-distance hauling. The figures quoted were specific, such as 25,000 pounds and 40,000 pounds. After the truckers had successfully lobbied the Pennsylvania legislature to raise the maximum limit to 60,000 pounds, which was commensurate with the limits in the adjoining states, the railroads hired a public relations agency to reverse the decision. The agency ran a statewide campaign, but it did not focus on the issue of the number of allowable pounds. Instead, it concentrated on creating an image of the truckers as "roadhogs" and raised issues that were highly ambiguous and in no way related to the specific dispute. The campaign was very successful in that it provided a sizable public response from outraged motorists who resented the large trucks on the road. Eventually, the Governor of Pennsylvania had to veto the bill because of the adverse public reaction, even though he personally favored its passage.[5]

The trucking conflict was successfully expanded by turning a highly specific conflict into a very general issue, a typical ploy of the public relations agency when it enters the fray. This does not mean that specifics can never aid one's cause. Under certain conditions,

---

[4] The reverse of the proposition would be: the greater the extent to which an issue can be defined concretely, the greater the likelihood that the conflict will be privatized (that is, not extended to a larger public). We endorse the reverse set of linkages, attempting to explain why conflicts do not become expanded to larger groups. Occasionally, references will be made in the text to processes narrowing conflicts as well as enlarging them. However, our primary emphasis is on conflict expansion.

[5] Andrew Hacker, "Pressure Politics in Pennsylvania: The Truckers vs. the Railroads," in Alan Westin (ed.), *The Uses of Power: 7 Cases in American Politics* (New York: Harcourt, 1962), pp. 326–77.

specific quantities can be of benefit even when they have no basis in fact.

For example, the State Department and the newspaper correspondents successfully redefined the Dominican revolt in 1965 as a "Communist guessing-game" and used an unsubstantiated number of Communists to justify a particular action. However, the primary justification in such cases is not the specific quantities; they are merely used as proof of a more general process that is at work, in this case, the "Communist conspiracy." [6]

Thus, while numbers are utilized in such an instance, they are merely a means of justifying the larger, more ambiguous social process at work. Senator Joseph McCarthy, in his search for conspirators in the government, occasionally identified X number of conspirators in the State Department. However, the number constantly varied, and his principal purpose was not a "numbers game," but a campaign to make the public aware of the larger, more dangerous issue.

The tenor of McCarthy's campaign is shown in his first speech, designed to gain visibility for his cause.

> The reason why we find ourselves in a position of impotency is not because our only potential enemy has sent men to invade our shores, but rather because of the traitorous actions of those who have been treated so well by this nation. . . . [Those] who have been selling this nation out . . . have had . . . the finest homes, the finest college educations, and the finest jobs in the government. This is glaringly true in the State Department. They're the bright young men who are born with silver spoons in their mouths who are the ones with the worst records.[7]

Thus, McCarthy usually did not get more specific than the State Department and a "State Department type," a prototype of all that was wrong with our foreign policy. But he was concerned with a general broadside attack on the institutions of government, even when he was delineating specific aspects of the problem or identifying specific individuals. Indeed, when he had to become specific in the Peress case during the Army-McCarthy hearings, he suffered a loss of pub-

[6] See Theodore Draper, *The Dominican Crisis* (New York: Commentary Reports, 1968), pp. 159–74.
[7] Joseph McCarthy, *Congressional Record,* February 20, 1950, p. 1954.

lic support. The cause was the most successful when it was defined as a broad issue of unspecified conspiracy.

The concreteness-specificity continuum can be approached from a variety of perspectives. For example, James Wilson distinguishes between a group's goal and its principles. Any successful campaign must combine the two ingredients.

The Poor People's Campaign of 1968 was undertaken to eliminate hunger. However, even such a goal may be defined narrowly or broadly. There are a variety of channels that could be utilized to attain such an objective, and there are a number of ways of phrasing the objective, but with different implications. Thus, an aim is "specific" in that it delineates an objective, but it does not specify a range of alternatives desired, nor does it adequately define the problem.

Under the heading of "goals," Wilson discussed a number of criteria for evaluating objectives. Goals could be either positive or negative and could involve the welfare or the status of the group. A welfare goal would involve some tangible objective such as voting rights; a status objective would be intangible, such as a promise to eliminate barriers to minority groups. A group focusing on welfare objectives would have a better chance of mobilizing adherents simply because the people could identify the issue more clearly.

The second aspect of the problem, according to Wilson, is the broad principle that lies behind the objective. He observes that:

> the specific goal is always related to a general, more vague principle. Each specific goal is the immediately sought application of some general notion concerning equality, opportunity, or status. This is essential, inasmuch as such principles are an essential incentive with which to mobilize large numbers of contributors to the protest action. Few will benefit personally from the attainment of the specific goal; therefore, general reasons of an ethical character must be offered to attract the support of the many.[8]

The distinction between goals and principles is not rigid, nor is it that relevant to the study of agenda-building except in terms of the things leaders emphasize during the course of a controversy. The im-

[8] James Wilson, "The Strategy of Protest: Problems of Negro Civic Action," *Journal of Conflict Resolution* 5 (1961), p. 93. For a review of Wilson's position see JCR, pp. 291–303.

portant question is how issue *X* is defined—whether it is done primarily by vague symbols such as *liberty* and *equality* or by more specific objectives. If the leaders define the issue specifically in terms of certain objectives, then the issue is classified as *concrete*. Most successful issue campaigns stress some type of goal, but that is often difficult given a variety of interpretations to keep the campaign as attractive as possible to a diverse group of onlookers. For example, the Prohibition movement had a specific goal, but it became somewhat confused. The leaders changed their objectives at various times, affecting the size of their audience, and it was difficult at times to ascertain what their objectives were.[9]

Thus, when Wilson writes that a prerequisite of mass action is an "agreed upon goal on behalf of which mass action can be mobilized," [10] we would reply that there has to be some type of motivating force to bring individuals together seeking some objective. But that the objective is specific enough to be called a "goal" or that all members assume the same definition as the leaders is open to question. To use Wilson's terminology, goals can become as diffuse as principles. The ultimate goals are not clear in the initial statement of the issue; they become defined in the course of the campaign.

As a result, the issue is more likely to be expanded when it is defined so broadly that everyone can find a cause in the campaign that he likes and can identify with. The utilization of specifics in the cause is often significant and is usually misleading. When one stresses a great number of specific facts and makes a concrete case, the experience can be deflating. This has often happened on the fluoridation issue.[11]

The only disadvantage to waging an ambiguous public campaign is that ultimately, a group must make specific demands. Otherwise, a decision-maker can successfully keep a grievance off the agenda by complaining that "they [the group in question] did not know what they wanted, so how could I act?" This charge is often used against

[9] For example, see Margaret Nelson, "Prohibition: A Case Study in Societal Misguidance," *American Behavioral Scientist* 12 (1968), pp. 37–42; and James Timberlake, *Prohibition and the Progressive Movement* (Cambridge: Harvard University Press, 1963), passim.

[10] Wilson, *op. cit.*, p. 293.

[11] William Gamson, "The Fluoridation Dialogue," *Public Opinion Quarterly* 25 (1961), pp. 526–37.

groups that seek to end poverty. Often their grievance becomes so abstruse that decision-makers are confused as to the type of action desired.

SOCIAL SIGNIFICANCE.   Another characteristic of an issue that will help determine the likelihood of its exposure to an enlarged audience is its social significance. *The more socially significant an issue is defined to be, the greater the likelihood that it will be expanded to a larger public.*

Issues that are concerned with the basic welfare of most people or a substantial segment of the populace would be included (for example, welfare programs). Also involved would be efforts to upgrade the conditions of large urban masses. An example of an attempt to make an issue socially significant was the following appeal by an official of the Women's Strike for Peace: "You must have to feel when you look at children—regardless of their color or condition—the hope that they'll go on forever . . . . Feeling so, you shout NO! to annihilation for the species. Presto you're a Woman for Peace." [12] However, the Women's Strike for Peace has been unable to mobilize a large segment of the populace toward a socially significant objective because its issue was redefined in terms of subversion. The organization was alleged to have "Communist leaning" members, and the group was investigated by the House Un-American Activities Committee, with no consideration being given its proposals to achieve peace.

The above example demonstrates that the alleged "social significance" of a cause may not be enough in itself to guarantee expansion to a larger populace. Often, people with significant problems and programs have been denied access for decades. This indicates that more than one characteristic must be present to insure a visible issue. The interplay of the various issue characteristics and the time interval in which the issue develops are crucial in determining whether or not the issue makes an institutional agenda.

To illustrate further the problems associated with expanding socially significant issues, consider the march on Washington by civil rights groups in the summer of 1968. The reasons for the march were certainly defined in socially significant terms.

[12] Esther Garst, "Women: Middle Class Masses," *Fellowship* (November 1, 1967), pp. 11–12.

We march to redeem the American promise. . . . Is there a meaningful right to life when the Department of Agriculture tells us that nearly 20 million Americans are deprived of necessary nutrition . . . ? Is there genuine liberty when economic misery turns millions into outcasts . . . [who] do not even . . . vote? 92% of the hungry citizens are excluded from the Federal Government's basic food program.[13]

It is certainly true that most Americans regard the hungry as a social problem and feel that they must be fed even at governmental expense. In this instance, however, that belief was not enough to expand the issue, because Americans also believe that everyone should take care of his own problems and be able to feed himself, unless he is sick or physically handicapped. In addition, there is a popular stereotype of blacks as lazy people who will not try to better themselves. Whites who believe that stereotype ask Why give them a governmental dole when they do not even make an attempt to become self-sufficient? Since most of the poor in the above issue were black, people focused on whether the blacks deserved public aid rather than on the social significance of the cause.

The Harris poll reported that 56 percent of the American public (61 percent of the whites) "did not feel in sympathy with what the Poor People's March is trying to do." [14] As a consequence, the ensuing march did not expand the issue to a larger public, and the entire campaign was less than a success.[15]

TEMPORAL RELEVANCE. If an issue has long-term implications beyond the exigencies of the immediate situation, there is a greater likelihood that it will attain additional visibility. In propositional form: *the more that an issue is defined as having extended temporal relevance, the greater the chance that it will be exposed to a larger audience.*

This characteristic figures prominently in a hassle concerning possible grants from the government. The groups who want money say

[13] Mobilization Committee, "A Call to Americans of Good Will to Join a National Mobilization in Support of the Poor People's Campaign," May, 1968.
[14] Louis Harris, "Negroes for, Whites against, poor drive." *Washington Post,* June 10, 1968, p. A7.
[15] For a review of the events leading to the march and their aftermath, see Carolyn Atkinson, "Coalition Building and Mobilization Against Poverty," *American Behavioral Scientist* 12 No. 2 (1968), pp. 48–52.

that systematic exclusion will have long-run implications that will be damaging to individuals and their offspring; those who oppose such grants argue that once a collectivity is given a governmental subsidy of some sort, it will be very difficult to deny similar grants in the future.

The fight over aid to parochial schools has focused on this dimension. Catholic officials argue that denial of public funds will result in serious educational deficiencies having economic, social, and cultural implications for the deprived students. Opponents argue that the spillover into future doles is a dangerous precedent. For example, in 1961, C. Stanley Lowell, director of an organization created to deny public funding for parochial education, made the following statement:

> I should like to call attention to the end result of a program of grants to church schools or loans to church schools. Once the Congress reverses our tradition and embarks upon such a course, it will find that turning back is extremely difficult. The movement tends to be the other way. From small loans to large grants, so the process unfolds until the taxpayers are charged with the entire bill for these schools.[16]

The above example illustrates that temporal relevance can be defined in terms of the likelihood of spillover, or additional consequences for others.

Another example illustrating the nature of "spillover" is the dialogue concerning the continuation of the Vietnam war. As one of their major arguments, opponents of the war have stressed its temporal relevance. They say that in addition to the injustices to the Vietnamese, a major reason for halting the conflict is the likelihood that "future Vietnams" are going to occur in Southeast Asia until the United States learns to deal with civil discord in an underdeveloped state.

The war also illustrates another aspect of temporal relevance. Once the nation was engaged in a war of allegedly "limited proportions," it became very difficult to maintain the conflict at a given

---

[16] Hugh Douglas Price, "Schools, Scholarships and Congressmen: The Kennedy Aid to Education Program," in Alan Westin (ed.), *The Centers of Power: 3 Cases in American National Government* (New York: Harcourt, 1964), p. 65. For a complete review of the case, see Westin, pp. 54–105.

level. Appropriations and the scope of commitment necessarily increased in the fashion of Parkinson's Law. In this instance, skyrocketing costs precluded necessary expenditures in other issue areas such as the problems confronting the cities. Thus, the argument against a policy can be based on implications for future policies in that area or on the government's inability to control an approved program that works to the detriment of other programs.

The expansiveness of a governmental commitment is also illustrated in the conflict over whether appropriations for our space program are justified. The proponents of the program argue that it should be continued because of future payoffs: "(1) research and development payoffs that will have benefits on this planet; (2) payoffs from the earth-circling satellites; (3) payoffs that are dependent on man's traveling to outer space. . . ." [17] Opponents of the space program have had great difficulty in placing their criticism on the public agenda because the language of the space program proponents is always couched in "spillover" terms. As one observer wrote,

> The very words used—"fallout," "spinoff," or "by-product" to describe the process betray the oversimplification of many steps, translations and persons that an idea must travel through in order to be transferred from one use to another.[18]

A domestic issue that illustrates how an issue can be defined as temporally relevant to gain additional public support was the campaign to prohibit consumption of alcoholic beverages in the 1920's. In that instance, advocates of prohibition were working against a widespread belief that legalized alcohol was in the best interests of government. To overcome this belief, the issue was redefined in a number of ways. One was to show how it would affect the average citizen in the future. As one who studied the movement reported, "Prohibition would mean lowered taxes, since the middle class would no longer have to support asylums and jails filled with drunkards . . . prohibition would mean greater order and well-being during labor strikes." [19] More people became interested in the cause when it

---

[17] Edward Furash, "The Problem of Technology Transfer," in Bauer and Gergen, *op. cit.*, p. 312.
[18] *Ibid.*, p. 290.
[19] Nelson, *op. cit.*, p. 38.

was demonstrated to have considerable long run implications other than merely banning a certain category of beverages.[20]

COMPLEXITY. Another feature of an issue conflict is the extent to which an issue becomes defined as a technical, complex question in the debate over its merits. The proposition, we advance, asserts that *the more non-technical an issue is defined to be, the greater the likelihood that it will be expanded to a larger public.*[21]

An example that illustrates some of the ramifications of a complexity dimension was the fight over the Senate ratification of a treaty providing for a League of Nations following the First World War. After the cessation of hostilities, President Wilson returned to the United States from Paris and envisioned a world organization controlling the outbreak of future wars. Faced with an adamant Senate that balked at ratification of the treaty, he launched a nationwide trip to win the support of the general public, focusing on how the new world organization would preclude future global conflagrations. However, opponents in the Senate followed him around as a "truth squad" orating on a number of specific treaty provisions to which they took exception. This created a great deal of public confusion about the issue. The technicalization of the issue worked to the advantage of those who opposed the treaty. While the President tried to stress that the issue was basically "very simple," his opposition attempted to confuse the debate by bringing in a great number of details to limit public involvement and understanding.[22]

In the context of studying community conflicts, Peter Rossi writes:

---

[20] For a review of the controversy, see *Ibid.*, pp. 37–43; and Timberlake, *op. cit.*, passim.

[21] The reader must not confuse *concreteness* and *complexity*. *Concreteness* refers to the extent to which an issue is clearly delineated; *complexity* relates to the degree to which various facets of an issue are identified and discussed. An issue may be presented as *concrete*, but not necessarily as *complex*. For example, the Wilson campaign to make the United States a member of the League of Nations was a concrete issue, but to gain greater public support he did not make it a complex issue.

[22] For a review of Wilson's campaign to win support for the League of Nations, see Kurt Wimer, "A President Appeals to the People," in Rocco Tresolini and Richard Frost (eds.), *Case Studies in American National Government and Politics* (Englewood Cliffs: Prentice-Hall, 1966), pp. 123–30.

The strong temptation to designate an issue as "technical" . . . to be disposed of by administrative action is a recognition that on some matters it might be best to avoid coming before the bar of public opinion. Indeed, school administrators and public health officials may be regarded as prime advocates of this procedure which they have followed with great success.[23]

A study of attempts to pass fluoridation also illustrates the effect of complexity, since fluoridation is basically a "technical issue" that works to the disadvantage of its supporters when they attempt to expand the conflict. As one set of authors has noted:

Broad popular participation . . . spells defeat to fluoridation. It does so because fluoridation is a technical issue, the advantages of which are rather small from the citizen's point of view, . . . and because the opposition can easily implant doubt. No matter why it is discussed, . . . the opposition succeeds in arousing the citizenry.[24]

Another aspect of technicalization of an issue is the shroud of secrecy that can be invoked by decision-makers to avoid placing an item on the public agenda. Often, the governmental decision-makers reduce arguments about American involvement in the Vietnam conflict to a cost–effectiveness position, citing weapons superiority and body counts. Failing to win support with such positions, they argue that to become more technical would give the "enemy" too much of an advantage; therefore, they must invoke "national security grounds" and keep the debate on fairly simple terms. Opponents find it difficult to debate such a complex matter in terms easily understood by the public and are at a disadvantage when attempting to win popular support for anti-war programs.

Although the general proposition has merit, there are certain circumstances in which an issue will be expanded through the use of technical language. When a group might support a position and is highly knowledgeable in a certain area, it behooves supporters of an

[23] Peter Rossi, "Community Decision-Making," *Administrative Science Quarterly* 1 (1957), p. 430.
[24] Robert Crain, Elihu Katz, and Donald Rosenthal, *The Politics of Community Conflict: The Fluoridation Decision* (Indianapolis: Bobbs-Merrill, 1969), p. 228.

issue to define the conflict in terms that the potential supporters can understand. For example, the supporters of Prohibition made considerable headway in the business community because the issue was defined in fairly complex terms that the entrepreneurs were able to grasp. As one observer noted:

> The League [Anti-Saloon League] was also ready with economic arguments to swing big business to its side. In this effort, . . . the timing was propitious. . . . Scientific management became the vogue of industry, employers became vitally concerned with efficiency, and, subsequently, aware of its inverse relation to drink.[25]

CATEGORICAL PRECEDENCE. Another relevant element is the extent to which issues have been resolved in some similar fashion in the past. Lowi argues that this is the most important of all the issue characteristics. "Issues . . . are too ephemeral; it is on the basis of established expectation and a history of earlier government decisions of the same type that single issues are fought out." [26] In terms of a proposition, we state that *the more an issue is defined as lacking a clear precedent, the greater the chance that it will be expanded to a larger population.*

An example that illustrates the problem of precedence was the series of government imbroglios between the Justice Department and Southern school districts following the desegregation decision of 1954. When the Little Rock issue was raised, there were no clear precedents to support federal intervention. There was even disagreement within the Justice Department over whether or not it was proper for government to intervene in a local dispute. In such a situation, it was much easier to expand the conflict, since there were no clear guidelines on either side. Most of the populace was familiar with the case when the troop issue was publicized, with the Northern segment supporting the Eisenhower administration, and most Southern publics supporting the adamant stance of Governor Orval Faubus. In cases where precedents exist, it becomes more difficult for the disputants to enlarge the case beyond the initial disputants.[27]

[25] Nelson, *op. cit.,* p. 40.
[26] Theodore Lowi, "American Business, Public Policy, Case Studies and Political Theory," *World Politics* 16 (1964), p. 689.
[27] For a review of the circumstances surrounding the federal intervention into Central High School in Little Rock, see Corrine Silverman, "The Little Rock

Another aspect of the above dimension concerns the extent to which it is raised when it has no basis in fact. There may be a means of resolving a conflict, but if there is another issue at stake, one might expand the conflict by denying the existence of such procedures. This is, in essence, what happened in the strike of New York City public schools teachers in the fall of 1969. When a number of teachers were transferred from Ocean Hill-Brownsville to another area, Albert Shanker, head of the United Federation of Teachers (UFT), called a strike because the teachers were improperly assigned. However, such transfer procedures had been used in the past with no conflict. As Epstein noted, "Under the bylaws of the school system, a teacher may be transferred from one district to another. . . . In fact, 'hundreds of such transfers' . . . take place every year without the UFT objection." [28]

In this instance, Shanker was afraid of the potential power that could be mobilized by slum parents in a black area and successfully used the precedence issue as a basis for expanding the conflict. As one observer wrote: "Evidently the UFT chose to make an issue out of the Ocean Hill transfers . . . by raising the question of due process . . . to terrify its membership and thus prepare the way for a major strike." [29]

SUMMARY. Thus, all five characteristics discussed earlier have a bearing on the likelihood that a conflict will be expanded. Agreement by both parties on what characteristics will be emphasized in a dispute tends to restrict or expand the scope of the conflict. If the contending parties want to decide a question on the basis of social significance, with no clear precedent, their agreement should lead to an increase in the general visibility of the conflict as well as an increase in its intensity.

THE INTERVAL OF TIME. In addition to the five aspects of issues discussed above, there is another element that will help determine the extent to which a conflict will be expanded to a larger

---

Story," in Edwin Bock and Alan Campbell (eds.), *Case Studies in American Government* (Englewood Cliffs: Prentice-Hall, 1962), pp. 1–46.
[28] Jason Epstein, "The Issue at Ocean Hill," *The New York Review of Books,* Vol. 11 No. 9 (November 21, 1968), p. 3.
[29] *Ibid.*

audience. That is the length of time that is required before an issue can gain its ultimate scope: the mass public. We assert the following: *issues that gain the attention of the mass public must be developed rapidly.*

Conflicts that develop slowly over time may gain the visibility of the attention groups or the attentive public, but hardly ever will they get the attention of a larger audience. Conflicts that expand rapidly will be those with the greatest visibility. For example, the death of Senator Robert Kennedy brought the gun control issue to the attention of the nation within a matter of hours. Another example of a conflict with great visibility would be an important labor strike. A transportation strike, for instance, would develop rapidly and affect large numbers in urban centers, which in turn would lead to the need for extreme and drastic action by the parties involved.

Occasionally an issue may be defined very narrowly in the beginning and endure a long process in which its merits are debated. Then it may suddenly be redefined on an emotional basis and expand rapidly. For example, the Meredith case had a long life in the courts with little public reaction until the threat of Meredith's admission to a white school was credible to the Southern populace. Then there was an immediate emotional response.[30] Considering its duration, such an issue would appear to be an exception to our proposition. But if it is approached as an emotional issue, not an issue involving legal technicalities, then its rapid conversion into a "mass issue" would not be considered a deviant case. Thus a corollary to the proposition might read: *the quicker an issue can be converted into an emotional issue, the greater the likelihood that it will gain public visibility.*

Strategies for Conflict Containment

The impression that has been created thus far in the chapter is that there are only a few means by which conflicts can be contained; namely, by reversing the propositions presented above. However, there are a variety of strategies that the opponent can use to keep an issue off the agenda.[31] These strategies could be placed under the five

[30] For a review of the Meredith case, see Dean Alfange, "James H. Meredith, Transfer Student," in Tresolini and Frost, *op. cit.*, pp. 238–49.

[31] Opponents are those on the other side of the fence, which may include decision-makers in government. If decision-makers are actively opposed to a

characteristics of issues mentioned above, but explicit delineation of such strategies is necessary to give a more complete picture of the dynamics of agenda-building.

Two general dimensions can be used to categorize schemes designed to prevent issues from expanding. The first relates to the extent to which the strategy is group-oriented or issue-oriented. By *group-oriented,* we mean that the focus of attention is on the group itself, not the cause that it espouses. The alternative is an *issue-oriented* strategy wherein the concern is with the demands being made. For example, if Group A takes a stand on issue *X,* and the opponents say Group A is "Communist-dominated," the strategy is *group-oriented.* If, on the other hand, the opponents attack the merits of the issue stance of Group A as unrealistic, then the strategy would be considered *issue-oriented.*

Whereas the first dimension identifies the focal point of the strategy, the second refers to the tactics used. A group or an issue may be attacked directly or indirectly. A direct attack will focus on the merits or legitimacy of a group or the issue it is promoting. An indirect attack will avoid direct confrontation with the substantive merits or the legitimacy of a group or its demands.

Utilizing these two dimensions, we can identify four distinct types of strategy used by parties seeking to keep an issue off the agenda. The two by two table below shows these four types of strategy.

	GROUP-ORIENTED	ISSUE-ORIENTED
DIRECT	Attack Group	Defusing (of issue)
INDIRECT	Undermine Group	Blurring (of issue)

GROUP-ORIENTED STRATEGIES.　　There are two types of group-oriented strategies. The first involves attacking the opposing group directly to limit its appeal.

Perhaps the most prominent type of direct attack is *discrediting*

---

group's demands, they would enter the opposition and attempt to contain the conflict. Thus, opponents may include members of an affected governmental body.

the group. Examples include management discrediting the union movement and the general trend toward collectivization of the workers over the past few decades in conjunction with the dispute over the right-to-work laws. Another example would be the opponents of the American Civil Liberties Union characterizing the group as a "Communist front" or composed of "subversives."

A second tactic of group attack is *discrediting the leaders of a group*. An example of a leader attack is the assault anti-union groups made on James Hoffa following the sensational exposés produced by the McClellan Committee. Since Hoffa had little public sympathy at the time and was scornful toward non-Teamsters, discrediting him prevented union demands from getting on the agenda. It took a while for unions to live down the image of Hoffa as a prototype of all labor bosses.

A more current example of this tactic is seen in the grape controversy. The owners are critical not of the workers' attempt to unionize, but of their leader, Cesar Chavez. They say Chavez is a "rabble-rouser" interested in serving his own ends rather than those of the group. They believe they can win more support for their position by such criticism than by attacks on union organization efforts.

The second form of group-oriented strategy to constrain conflict is indirect. Opponents whittle away at a group's base of support, indirectly preventing expansion. One means is by *appeal over the heads of leaders to members*. Examples include the efforts by a national committee headed by John Glenn, who appealed to each member of the National Rifle Association to register his guns with the police. Another illustration is the effort to get support from individual doctors for Medicare during the battle in the early 1960's. A major ploy of Medicare supporters was to show that members of the opposition had come to accept their views.

A second indirect tactic is to *co-opt leaders*. This is a common strategy at the governmental level, and it can also be used in the private sphere. After the Detroit riot, the New Detroit Committee was created as a nongovernmental commission to aid minority groups in obtaining jobs in the automobile plants. The committee enlisted the aid of black leaders from the community. Black leaders were also co-opted in Los Angeles after the 1968 Watts riots. They helped create the Watts workshop, designed to help those in the ghetto release their frustrations through writing. Another illustration of co-opting is the effort to attain black capitalism without governmental subsidies, such as the North Philadelphia enclave sponsored by the Reverend Leon Sullivan. All of these attempts highlight the effort to publicize certain types of action by bringing dissidents into the structure in hopes of alleviating more serious grievances.

ISSUE-ORIENTED STRATEGIES. The other principal technique that can be used by groups to control the scope of the conflict focuses on issues, either directly or indirectly. When confronting an issue directly, the opponents recognize the issue as legitimate but deny its urgency and poignancy.

A common ploy is to provide *symbolic rewards or reassurance,* such as formal acceptance of petitions of grievances by guards outside the White House. When groups demonstrate against higher taxes at the state capitol, sympathetic statements from decision-makers will be reassuring. Even the mere fact that they are demonstrating at an important public site can be reinforcing to members of a group.

Another way of preventing conflict expansion is through *showcasing, or tokenism.* This ploy involves acting on a limited grievance in a larger problem. For example, a slum landlord may paint his dwellings, but make no repairs on the building. Another example is a real estate agency putting one black family in a previously all-white area to "integrate" it. Or a business might hire black M.B.A.'s and create junior executive positions for them, such as "Assistant Public Relations Manager for Community Affairs," to show that the company offers equal employment opportunities.

Issues may also be defused by *creating new organizational units to deal with a problem.* For example, at the national level, the creation of Cabinet posts for Transportation and for Health, Education and Welfare and the proposed establishment of a Department of Consumer Affairs represent little in the way of policy innovation, but give the impression of action. The same impression is created at the private level when a company sets up a labor grievance committee or a Real Estate Board sets up a study committee to investigate open housing. Peter Bachrach and Morton Baratz note that: "tactics such as these . . . are particularly effective when employed against impermanent or weakly organized groups (e.g., students, the poor) which have difficulty withstanding delay." [32]

A fourth way of confronting an issue directly is *anticipation,*

[32] Peter Bachrach and Morton Baratz, *Power and Poverty* (New York: Oxford, 1970), p. 45.

facing an important problem before public mobilization on the issue. This is done when some type of agenda position is likely if the problem is not forestalled. A business, anticipating that a union is going to want more money when a contract expires, might offer X amount of additional money, which is less than the union is likely to seek. The purpose would be to create a favorable climate of opinion for future dealings with the union and perhaps to persuade the union to accept less then they might otherwise demand. Another illustration of anticipation would involve a company located near the ghetto. The company might drop the high school diploma as a prerequisite for a job and institute large-scale training programs for blacks.

The second type of issue-oriented strategy is to confront the issue indirectly. Opponents sidestep the issue completely, making no effort to resolve the substantive aspects of the grievance. One technique is *symbol co-optation,* by which the opponents use the symbols of the adversary to preclude its seizing on a catchy phrase or gesture. Examples include the co-optation of "we shall overcome" and "tell it like it is" by disputants in conflicts far removed from civil rights controversy, in which the phrases were popularized initially. The poignancy of symbols can also be diluted inadvertently. For example, well meaning white liberals may unintentionally reduce the value of symbols like "soul" by co-opting them and using them out of context.

The loss of poignant symbols can pose severe problems for a group that is attempting to mobilize support. As Nicholas von Hoffman has written:

> One of the biggest problems facing the angry people who are thrashing around and coming up with new ideas is that the language but not the substance of their thought is stolen from them. President Nixon goes around making the V sign for peace. Flatulent politicians look you straight in the eye and begin their speeches by saying, "first, let's get down to the nitty gritty." This is disastrous to communication. If the top dog is going to bark like the underdog, how is the weaker of the two ever going to get his demands for justice and change understood.[33]

A second indirect tactic is *feigned constraint,* which takes the form of "I would like to help you but. . . ." For instance, a business-

[33] Nicholas von Hoffman, "The Showable and Sayable," *Washington Post,* March 10, 1969, p. B5.

man might tell representatives of the black community that he agrees that more jobs should be given to minority group members, but his training facilities are already taxed, so he cannot expand recruitment.

Another type of indirect confrontation is *postponement,* taking the grievance under advisement in an effort to seek out additional information. Opponents justify postponement on the grounds of inadequate prior information about a problem or simply the need to seek out more people before a solution is reached. The tobacco companies utilized this tactic when under attack by the American Cancer Association and other health groups. The responses by the automobile manufacturers to criticisms by Ralph Nader and other safety advocates are another example. A classic example of governmental use of this strategy is found in the establishment of special commissions and committees composed of notable people to investigate specific problems.

CONCLUSION. Thus, a variety of strategies can be used by a party to preclude the expansion of a conflict. Each of these strategies can be placed under the headings of the five issue categories discussed in this chapter. For example, groups trying to postpone action will discuss an issue in the context of temporal relevance, claiming that the issue is so important, adequate time must be spent canvassing alternative solutions to protect the lives of future citizens.

One of the key problems that remains is the role of language in issue expansion. To what extent are symbols relevant? What type of symbol dimensions aid in delineating the ramifications of issue enlargement? These questions are the focal points of the next chapter.

8

Symbol Utilization
and Conflict Expansion

We have delineated general propositions linking issue characteristics to the expansion of a dispute to involve greater numbers. But it is not enough merely to link the characteristics of a particular item to the size of the involved public, for the type of language used may be crucial in bringing the issue to public attention. In this chapter, we consider the types of symbols that are used by combatants to enlarge the scope of a particular conflict.

We propose that there is a set of linkages between the type of language that is used to define an issue to outsiders and the ultimate size of the audience that will become involved in the issue. This proposition is summarized in the following diagram:

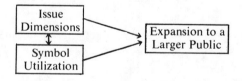

Before delineating a set of propositions concerning symbol utilization and the likelihood that an issue will be expanded to a larger public, we must clarify some assumptions. First, we assume that it is both possible and analytically useful to separate the symbol from its meaning. We do not assume that every citizen interprets a symbol the same way or even that symbols remain static. However, within a particular time context, certain symbols will be salient to most people and will provoke either positive or negative reactions.

For example, we are not concerned with how most people describe *Communism* or even how their conception relates to reality. Of concern is the general emotive response that such a symbol will evoke from most citizens. In this instance, the symbol is related, for most Americans, to *oppression, totalitarianism,* or other negative terms. The symbol has retained its emotive content with little alteration over the past two decades.

When analyzing symbols in the context of certain issue disputes, there are two principal questions that students of agenda-building must answer: (1) Is the symbol being used appropriately for the situation? [1] and (2) Is the application of the symbol appropriate to the subculture in which it is being used? Symbols must be relevant to the issue at hand; otherwise the public response will be one of confusion and ignorance. A symbol must also be relevant to the specific group toward which it is directed. For example, to use a symbol like *justice* for a group of suburban residents who are concerned with crime is to ignore their basic presumptions concerning law enforcement. While the symbol has system-level utility (that is, it has been used in the past), it may not relate to such a specific situation.

Symbol potency, or *symbol weight,* is influenced by the situation and by the people using it. The symbol must be appropriate for each instance and must appear to be the right type of language for a leader to utter at that time. The situation will depend on two elements: the nature of the combatants and the nature of the audience that might be added to either camp. Thus, language must be correct, not only for followers, but also for potential supporters. All of these elements are relevant when determining the impact of a series of symbols on a developing issue dispute.

In the various characteristics that will be discussed, emphasis is on the nature, not the content, of symbols. We are not so much concerned with what a particular symbol connotes as with the context in which it is used. Content will be considered as a category under the

[1] See Richard Merelman, "Learning and Legitimacy," *American Political Science Review* 58 (1964), pp. 553–57.

nature of symbols. As in the last chapter, we are asserting that certain types of symbols utilized in issue disputes will lead to the controversy's being enlarged to include persons not involved in the initial definition of the dispute.

Historical Precedence

The type of historical background supporting a symbol will be critical to its potency. The use of symbols with historical precedence will enhance the likelihood that a conflict can be expanded.

Groups involved in issue controversies may avail themselves of popular symbols that have been used over a long period of time by other groups and other decision-makers. Such symbols are recognized as having a certain type of meaning for the involved community. They can include terms leading to a positive emotive response, such as *liberty,* or those that lead to negative reactions, such as *police state* and *Communist-dominated*.

David Easton suggests that there are three levels of symbols in a system. The first applies to the government, or those personalities actually occupying positions at one point in time. The second refers to the regime that concerns formal and informal structures, "together with the rules of the game or codes of behavior that legitimate the actions of political authorities and specify what is expected of citizens." [2] The third refers to political community, symbols that "represent the members of society looked upon as a group of persons who seek to solve their problems in common through shared political structures." [3] Symbols concerned with historical precedence would involve community symbols such as *America, the flag, patriotism* and other terms that act as cohesive bonds for the entire nation.

Such symbols have two characteristics. First, they have scope. They have been applied to a great number of issue areas in the past. For example, the term *communist subversion* has been utilized by groups interested in a range of problems from Vietnam to fluoridation. Second, such symbols tend to evoke an intense reaction. A symbol such as *law and order* has meaning for most Americans today,

[2] David Easton and Robert Hess, "The Child's Political World," *Midwest Journal of Political Science* 6 (1962), p. 124.
[3] *Ibid*.

with all contending parties in most issue disputes trying to identify their cause with that cue.[4]

However, such symbols can vary with the passage of time. Symbols that had great appeal can die and lose their attraction. For example, the term *Indian* was once a great threat to whites, but it poses no threat today; *Communists* are the principal symbolic enemy at present. Thus, all symbols have temporal limitations. A term such as *black power* would have had no meaning a decade ago; now, however, it evokes a strong reaction from most blacks and whites.

Examples of the utilization of such community symbols are commonplace. Most issue disputes resolve in part around notions of *freedom, liberty, individual rights,* and *expanding power of the federal government.* Groups attempt to link disputes with the standard set of cues that have been developed in any community. Both sides have their favorite weapons regardless of the specific issue. For example, when discussing the role of the government in aiding schools, the proponents always refer to "federal aid" while opponents may characterize such a program as "federal control" that invites "interference from Washington."

As Hugh Douglas Price has written, "This sort of conflict [federal aid to schools] can still be handled, although it becomes difficult if the issues are framed in symbolic terms (*federal aid* versus *federal control*)." [5] However, the use of symbols with historical connotations is not, by itself, enough to expand a conflict. Thus, there must be other characteristics that are relevant to issue expansion.

Efficiency or Credibility of a Symbol

A symbol with public appeal will be used in a number of contexts. When symbols are used efficiently, there is a greater chance that the conflict will be expanded. However, with widespread use, a number of errors in usage can occur. Symbols may be used incorrectly, in that the symbol simply does not relate to issue content.

Incorrect usage of a symbol can lead to a decline in its credibil-

[4] This point will be modified in subsequent discussion in this chapter.

[5] Hugh Douglas Price, "Schools, Scholarships and Congressmen: The Kennedy Aid to Education Program," in Alan Westin (ed.), *The Centers of Power: 3 Cases in American National Government* (New York: Harcourt, 1964), p. 70.

ity. An illustration would be the emphasis on the symbols of *victory* and *the troops will be home by Christmas* by the American decision-makers during the early phases of the Vietnam war. Early in the conflict, these symbols had great utility and were important in mobilizing support for the war on the home front. However, when it became apparent to the mass public that victory in the sense of military conquest of the Vietnam land mass was unlikely, these symbols lost their credibility.

Another type of situation involves the credibility of symbols that have factual bases but carry connotations that are potentially inflammatory. The controversy surrounding the Moynihan Report illustrates that situation. In early 1965, the Johnson administration was looking for legislative alternatives to deal with the problem of urban poverty. Daniel Moynihan produced a report that suggested family welfare as a referent for evaluating the desirability of particular poverty programs.

The Moynihan Report stressed the importance of family stability in determining the success of future urban ghetto programs. It noted that the Negro family was on the verge of disintegration and that progress was unlikely until the family was made a viable social unit. The initial reaction to the Report was mixed; but then black civil rights leaders began to fixate on the symbol of the *Negro family*. To them, it was a negative aphorism that reflected the stereotypes of white society.

For example, Floyd McKissick, the director of CORE, said:

> Just because Moynihan believes in the middle class values doesn't mean that they are the best for everyone. . . . [He] thinks everyone should have a family structure like his own. . . . [He] also emphasizes the negative aspects of the Negroes.[6]

According to Bayard Rustin:

> It [the Report] left people with the view that this was a complete and perfectly true picture of the Negro families. . . . We must talk about the poor family, not simply the Negro family. Poverty is a problem. It is amazing that Negro families exist at all.[7]

[6] Lee Rainwater and William Yancey, *The Moynihan Report and the Politics of Controversy* (Cambridge: MIT Press, 1967), p. 200.
[7] *Ibid.*

James Farmer attacked the Report as providing "the fuel for a new racism." [8]

Faced with the strong attack by civil rights leaders, Secretary of Labor Willard Wirtz attempted to redefine the situation: "I think you'll find earlier emphasis . . . on the economic need for jobs, the broader need for education . . . rather than any extensive attention directed at the family as such." [9]

Nonetheless, the whole battle surrounding the Moynihan Report tended to focus on the symbol of the *Negro family* and its negative connotations. Little attention was directed at other facets of the Report. As a consequence, the government was unable to use the Report as the basis for mobilization of support of new urban programs.

Incorrect usage can occur at any level. The error is exacerbated when symbols are used to support predictions that fail to materialize, when proponents continue to use symbols that have been discredited, or when most people recognize that a symbol has been misapplied from the very beginning.

Symbolic Saturation

The extent of symbolic differentiation within the community will also influence the nature of a symbol's appeals. The problem is that the symbol may be utilized for so many causes, it begins to lose its utility for any specific case. A community can become so saturated with a symbol that it becomes difficult for people to ascertain the specific relationship between the symbol and the issue at hand. Thus, when the proponents of an issue position draw upon symbols that have not saturated the community, they are more likely to expand the conflict to a larger public.

Overuse can take two forms. A symbol might be used in many different types of contexts, or it might be used too frequently in one context.

In the early days of the civil rights movement, demonstrators effectively utilized symbols like *police brutality,* and *human rights* to attract many whites who empathized with their plight. However, con-

[8] *Ibid.*, p. 258.
[9] *Ibid.*, pp. 259–60. For a complete review of the controversy, see *Ibid.*, chapters 5–14.

frontations with the law became more numerous and spread beyond the South, and the symbols began to lose their utility in mobilizing support. In fact, overuse has led many whites to react negatively to symbols such as *police brutality*.

Another symbol that is currently very popular in local controversies and that may soon face the danger of saturation is *decentralization*. In the New York school controversy of the autumn of 1968, this term was utilized very effectively by the teachers' union. The teachers were able to define *decentralization* to mean "community control and [that] means that blacks and Puerto Ricans will control millions of dollars." [10] The term was also used to arouse "the fear that from New York's pathetic ghettos there has arisen a monster which threatens not only the jobs of the trade unionists but the very lives of the city's Jews." [11] However, since the New York controversy, *decentralization* has been used in so many cases, it is doubtful that it will retain its potency as a mobilization symbol.

Similarly, national symbols may become so widely used over time that they have no bearing on the public's view of specific cases. For example, in the debate over whether foreign aid should be given to specific countries, proponents frequently tie their argument to the symbol of the *national interest*. However, it is unlikely that the average person will see any relationship between gratuitous investment in another country's economy and significant foreign policy interests of the United States. As a consequence, proponents will have difficulty gaining large public support for this program, unless they use other symbols to promote it.[12]

Symbolic Reinforcement

Another aspect of the symbolic structuring of an issue position to win outside support involves the notion of reinforcement. One must

[10] Jason Epstein, "The Issue at Ocean Hill," *New York Review of Books,* 11 No. 9 (November 21, 1968), p. 4.
[11] *Ibid.*
[12] Theodore Geiger and Robert Hansen, "The Role of Information in Decision-Making on Foreign Aid," in Raymond Bauer and Kenneth Gergen (eds.), *The Study of Policy Formation* (New York: Free Press, 1968), pp. 341–45.

look not only at the key symbols, but also at the whole range of aux-iliary symbols that are used and at the context in which they are used to determine whether or not an appeal is likely to advance the issue stance of a particular group. When symbolic reinforcement is pres-ent, it is more likely that an issue position can be expanded.

One way in which a cause is reinforced is through the associa-tion of issue-specific symbols with other symbols salient to the com-munity. For example, in the New York City school strike, Albert Shanker, head of the UFT, stressed one symbol primarily—the de-nial of *due process* for certain teachers. The symbol had historical precedence and seemed credible, since most people could see that the Ocean Hill teachers were dismissed without adequate procedures to protect them. But Shanker also used other terms, such as *firings* and *forced removals,* to describe the transfers. Such symbols attracted supporters from New York City's laboring ranks, particularly public servants. Shanker also asserted that such a precedent would lead to a complete breakdown of the school system. Symbols like *chaos* and *fragmentation* were constantly utilized to impress upon the public the gravity of the situation. Such a wide-based symbolic assault was cal-culated to win the support of a wide variety of the city's residents.

However, the key symbol that brought immediate support from specific attention groups (such as the Anti-Defamation League) and a more diffuse attention public (Jewish residents of the city) was that of *anti-Semitism.* Since most of the teachers in the city were Jewish, such a symbol implied that there was a conspiracy afoot to dismiss all of the Jewish teachers or remove them to less desirable jobs. Thus, Shanker and his associates utilized a wide variety of symbols that attracted a great deal of outside support. Such a use of symbols was perhaps essential, since the conflict occurred in a potentially highly emotive context. A strike of such magnitude could have aroused the animosity of all parents with children in the city's schools.[13]

Another aspect of the phenomenon of reinforcement relates to the nature of the person utilizing the symbol. Often, the impact of a symbol will be enhanced when it is used by a person the public rec-ognizes. A prime example is the simple presence of the Reverend

[13] Epstein, *op. cit.,* pp. 3, 4, 44.

Martin Luther King and his impact on a controversy. As one observer noted, "King must be counted as one of the primary assets of the poor. His mere association with a cause was often enough to grant it sufficient legitimacy to assure massive support." [14]

King built a basis of support over a long period of time. Occasionally, however, a man can create support by one action that lifts him into public prominence. Bayard Rustin, for example, gained great prestige among the informed segment of the populace by organizing the civil rights march on Washington in 1963. His presence added support to the march on Washington in the summer of 1968. As one writer observed, "His considerable expertise in and reputation for mobilizing effective and non-violent demonstrations were assets of [such] power that . . . organizations . . . committed their assets to Rustin for the poor before knowing the details of his plans." [15] His resignation from the march reduced the amount of outside support from the non-poor.

Often, when a group is attempting to force its demands onto a governmental agenda, the person making the demand will be critical. For example, when Stokely Carmichael threatened the white power structure of a particular city with certain corrective actions if no progress was made, the threat had greater credibility than it would have had if voiced by a local black official. Onlookers judge the veracity of the espouser as well as the content of the message.

Another source of reinforcement is the position of the person using the symbol. Certain positions are endowed with respect that adds support for a cause. For example, the Christian Anti-Communist Crusade always espoused strong anti-Communist views, but its claims were not legitimized until an ex-agent for the Federal Bureau of Investigation became a member. Since the FBI was considered the ultimate authority in dealing with subversion, a former agent's affiliation with the crusade lent respectability and prestige to its cause. Thus symbolic reinforcement may involve the past background of those espousing issue positions as well as the range of the symbols that are used.

[14] Carolyn Atkinson, "Coalition Building and Mobilization Against Poverty," *American Behavioral Scientist* 12 (1968), p. 49.
[15] *Ibid.*, p. 50.

Urgency Portent of a Symbol

Symbols that have action content are more likely to be effective than symbols that have no behavioral portent. When symbols stress urgent actions, conflicts are more likely to be expanded.

There are two characteristics of the *urgency portent* dimension. The first involves the words themselves. Symbols such as *Freedom Now* have an advantage because they connote a specific time commitment to action. If one is attempting to mobilize a public against some outside threat, one must emphasize the rapidity with which the opponent is gaining strength and becoming a more salient threat. For example, supporters of the Vietnam conflict utilize this tactic by referring to the immediacy of the Communist menace spilling over to Honolulu and to southern California if it is not stopped in South Vietnam.

Another example involves the Blaine Amendment controversy in New York in 1967. The Blaine Amendment referred to a provision in the State Constitution that banned any state aid to parochial schools. It became a major issue in the 1967 election campaign, and both sides utilized threat symbols suggesting a specific action commitment. Americans United, a group strongly opposed to such aid, stressed the theme of *Wake Up New York* and made an "emergency alert" appeal to the mass of the state for funds and assistance to help preclude passage of aid to parochial schools. This exacerbated public concern, and the issue was the most bitterly contested in the campaign.[16]

The context or setting in which a symbol is used will also bear on its action portent. A cry of "get whitey" is more likely to be a spur to action when uttered by a black man on a crowded ghetto

[16] For a review of the campaign, see Richard Morgan, *The Politics of Religious Conflict: Church and State in America* (New York: Pegasus, 1968), pp. 98–127. The stress on urgent action, or giving the impression that some type of action is being taken or is required, is similar to Murray Edelman's thesis that the criterion that determines the success of a leader is the extent to which he is creating the impression that he is coping with problems. See Edelman, *The Symbolic Uses of Politics* (Urbana: University of Illinois Press, 1964), pp. 73–94.

street in front of a store with a white proprietor than when shouted at a passing motorist.

Conclusion

In this chapter, we have reviewed how the nature of a symbolic cue can be instrumental in the expansion of a dispute. The five dimensions of symbolic usage that we have considered, when viewed in conjunction with the five characteristics of an issue delineated earlier, provide a more complete picture of the dynamics of issue expansion.

The next question is the extent to which one can identify different strategies through which groups seek to place an issue on the docket. The types of symbols employed will play a key role in determining these strategies. Another key element is the role of the mass media in the diffusion of an issue to various publics. These subjects will receive attention in the next chapter.

9

The Functions of Symbols
and the Mass Media
in Issue Expansion

In the previous chapter, the relationship between symbols and issue expansion was discussed. However, the interplay of symbols in finally placing an issue on the public docket has many more ramifications. Most important is how symbols are channeled into different types of strategy for achieving specific objectives.

This chapter focuses on the dynamic interplay between symbol usage and the techniques that groups utilize to gain and direct supportive public attention. The mass media plays a pivotal role in highlighting this interplay and in determining the success of an issue.[1] As Norton Long has written, "To a large extent, it [the press] sets the civic agenda."[2] The following diagram illustrates the intermediary role of the mass media:

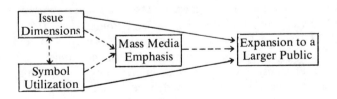

[1] Michael Lipsky, "Protest as a Political Resource," *American Political Science Review* 62 (1968), pp. 1151–53.
[2] Norton Long, "The Local Community as an Ecology of Games," *American Journal of Sociology* 44 (1958), p. 260.

There are five different strategies that parties in conflicts use to enlarge the controversy and muster support. Symbols are used for different purposes—externally, to influence the onlookers and the relevant decision-makers; internally, to encourage the group committed to fight for a particular cause.

Arousal

The first strategy that symbols reinforce is arousal, the activation of heretofore latent support from the community. This strategy was reflected in the previous chapter, which stressed the ways that groups could expand concern for an issue. Herbert Blumer aptly describes this process: "This [expansion] takes place through a process in which attention has to be gained, interests awakened, grievances exploited, ideas implanted, doubts dispelled, feelings aroused, new objects created, and new perspectives developed." [3]

The mass media will play an important part in determining the success of arousal. Dependence on the media for spreading symbols to the larger public increases with the expanding scope of conflict. Thus, the media will play a more important role with greater arousal than merely creating an atmosphere for favorable reception. Arousal feeds on itself and tends to snowball. When the media take an interest in a situation they usually follow up on it, generating greater and greater attention and concern. Media can artificially generate interest and tend to perpetuate this concern once the issue gains a larger audience.

This fact is illustrated in the following example: In the summer of 1968, Walter Headley, the Miami chief of police, announced a crackdown on crime in the ghettos. The story was reported in the *Miami Herald* with the headline, "Miami Police Start 'Get Tough' Policy." [4] The paper quoted the police chief as saying, "My men will use shotguns, guns, and a get-tough policy in the slums. . . . [The police department] is declaring war on criminals . . . [who as] felons will learn that they can't be bonded out from the morgue." [5]

[3] Herbert Blumer, "Collective Behavior," in J. B. Gittler (ed.), *Review of Sociology* (New York: Wiley, 1957), p. 148.
[4] *The Miami Report*. Washington, D.C.: United States Government Printing Office, 1969, p. 33.
[5] *Ibid*.

This policy statement brought a wave of protest from black leaders and civil libertarian organizations. They demanded that the new policy be placed on the agenda of the Miami City Council for a complete review. One community leader from the ghetto said, "If you want to have a riot, let'em start stopping and frisking and shooting people. . . . There's no disagreement that we need good law enforcement. There are some trigger-happy policemen waiting for this kind of thing." [6] The mass media in the Miami area and throughout the nation focused on this exchange of conflicting statements over the proper way of handling the increasing incidence of crime. The press in the Miami area overwhelmingly placed the police chief in a favorable light, and he was supported by many telegrams as well as by printed statements from ghetto residents. A favorite theme of the media was that Headley could not sleep nights because of the high crime rate and he felt that he had to act. [7]

Eventually, the issue was placed on the formal agenda, but no action was taken. Indeed there was no evidence that the symbolic crusade against crime in the media had any impact on the number of crimes committed in the ghetto, although the arrest rate did increase. However, the media were instrumental in arousing support for the police chief against the outcries of a few outraged citizens who believed that the crackdown was likely to impair rather than improve conditions in the ghetto.

The media ordinarily are not the initiators of arousal. A group must gain some initial success before the media will focus on an issue. Once the media take an interest in a controversy, however, they will often play an important role in reinforcing or altering the prevailing definition of the conflict.

Examples of media participation in arousal are numerous. Few are more dramatic than the role the Hearst newspapers played in the ultimate declaration of war on Spain just before the turn of the century. Another notable example was the part "elite newspapers" such as the *New York Times* played in publicizing the success of conservative groups in promoting a constitutional convention to consider proposals to limit the power of the Supreme Court in the early 1960's. The proposals included a recommendation for the creation of a Court of the Union, composed of the chief justices of the fifty state supreme courts, which would convene annually to review the deci-

[6] *Ibid.*, p. 41.
[7] *Ibid.*, p. 34. For a complete review of the media coverage, see pp. 1–47.

sions of the Supreme Court. When the newspapers publicized the fact that the proposal had passed numerous state legislatures and was nearing the number required for the calling of a constitutional convention, the furor that was aroused killed the proposal in other state legislatures and prevented a major constitutional question from developing.

When a group is attempting to win support for their position, arousal is the first ploy they will normally use. If that is unsuccessful, they will use other tactics.

Provocation

Another strategy with the ultimate objective of forcing agenda inclusion is provocation, in which a group takes a certain action designed to provoke another group into action. The latter group's reaction will enable the initiating group to attain greater publicity and sympathy. This strategy was employed by the peace marchers in the summer of 1968 when they sought to provoke the Chicago police at the Democratic National Convention into some type of violent reaction that would win support for the demonstrators.

The success of such confrontation tactics will vary from issue to issue. As the Walker Report noted on the Chicago violence, "The disruptive tactics . . . were intended to expose the inhumanity . . . hypocrisy or militaristic repression with which dissenters take issue." [8] The violence against mass media representatives eventually helped win a favorable treatment of the demonstrators' action in front of a nation of onlookers. Nonetheless, the immediate response was not new support for the demonstrators but a strong public reaction against their tactics. Only after the issuance of the Walker Report, which indicated that there had been a repressive police response, did the public reaction mellow toward the demonstrators.

An example of a more successful use of provocation is found in the civil rights movement of the early 1960's. The civil rights groups always selected the "roughest town" or the one in which they expected the most brutal police repression so that their cause would be aided by a national revulsion against such tactics. Such was the rea-

[8] *The Walker Report: Rights in Conflict* (New York: Bantam Books, 1968), p. 18.

soning behind the selection of Selma, Alabama, and the confrontation with Police Chief Eugene "Bull" Connor. The brutality against Selma demonstrators was instrumental in the subsequent placing of black grievances on the agenda of the federal government.

Another aspect of provocation concerns the choice of language and symbols in which to couch an issue. Often the use of obscene language and the profaning of salient community symbols will provoke a strong response from the target groups that may enable the initiators to win more support. For example, college demonstrators use obscene language in the hope of provoking a response from the college administration that will bring other students to their cause on the basis of upholding free speech. The use of obscene language has the additional advantage of concealing real demands; therefore, it can serve as a strong bargaining tool on behalf of the activists. As von Hoffman notes: "The judicious use of four letter words restores meaning to what the politicians . . . call dialogue. Obscenity sets up the possibility of having real discussions about real disagreements because dirty words make it impossible to disguise disagreement and claim consensus where none exists." [9]

Ordinarily, provocation is utilized when arousal fails, at least in the estimation of the issue leaders. If arousal is successful, leaders will be less likely to resort to provocative tactics. Provocation is also used when an adversary is successful at arousal. For example, opponents of the civil rights movement have asserted that the movement is "Communistic" or "Communist-inspired," knowing full well that their assertion would prompt leaders of the American Communist Party to issue statements expressing support for the civil rights movement and acknowledging participation in sit-ins and picket lines. Given such a surfeit of symbols, the opponents then claimed evidence of subversive groups at work in the movement.

Success is not always guaranteed when such a strategy is employed. New Orleans District Attorney Jim Garrison utilized a number of emotive symbols in attempting to discredit the Warren Commission Report; for example, *the expanding power of the federal government, cover-up by top leaders,* and *suppression of information by President Johnson.* In this manner, he hoped to elicit a response

[9] Nicholas von Hoffman, "The Showable and Sayable," *Washington Post,* March 10, 1969, p. B5.

by the governmental agencies and personalities involved (particularly the Central Intelligence Agency and the Federal Bureau of Investigation) so that he could engage in a public dialogue and thereby build a basis of support. However, no such response was forthcoming, and he could only assert that official silence indicated the weakness of the government's case. Finally, he attempted to bring the governmental decision-makers into the debate through a trial charging an individual with complicity in the crime, but again he was unsuccessful.

Provocation can serve internal as well as external needs of a group. Often, provoking another group to respond can promote cohesion in one's own group and solidify supporters. The aggressive response of the police to the Black Panthers of Newark has been used by the Panthers to promote greater hatred of the police in the black ghetto and thereby to enhance the standing of the Panthers with blacks in the area.[10]

Such tactics can win immediate response from political decision-makers. Not only do the Panthers win support from the black community when they antagonize the police into repressive counter-attacks, but they also demonstrate that they are a credible threat to governmental authorities. The fact that they can mobilize support from their own community and frighten the whites by manipulating the frequency and level of police response gives them great viability and considerable bargaining power. As Ross Baker writes:

> It would be difficult for them to present themselves as "responsible spokesmen" of the black community. But this is precisely the image the Panthers hope to achieve, for they see their role as "irresponsible spokesmen" as an infinitely more productive approach. That the Panthers prefer to use threats and menacing gestures is less a commentary on black extremism than it is on the unresponsiveness of whites.[11]

The mass media will also play an important role in provocation. The distinctive feature of this strategy is that it will lead the mass media to seek out the issues and issue leaders. In all other situations, the issue leaders will generally have to seek out the mass media. For

[10] Ross Baker, "A New Breed of Panther," *Washington Post*, March 2, 1969, p. B2.
[11] *Ibid.*

example, the Chicago demonstrators received wide attention as soon as it was clear that confrontation with the authorities was part of the strategy.

Often, a group will resort to provocative tactics because the press is reluctant to focus on its arousal tactics. Through provocation, the issue leaders can make an event newsworthy and force the mass media to cover it. The success of provocation in capturing media attention is due to its potential for the sensational, the violent, and the dramatic—qualities that will appeal to the readers and viewers of the media. Issue groups are more dependent on the press when using provocation than when using any other strategy. For example, the press was in large part responsible for encouraging the belief that black guerilla raids were to blame for inciting major outbreaks of urban violence, although the facts suggest that these outbursts were spontaneous. One report criticized the press for provocation through "imprecise, distorted and inaccurate reporting." [12] With respect to the violence in Cleveland in the summer of 1969, the same study found that the press stressed the "theme of a deliberate plot against the police. . . . What is surprising is that the press, particularly at the national level, showed so little initiative with regard to checking and investigating such disorders further." [13] Later reports showed that the outburst in Cleveland was most probably spontaneous.[14]

Another example of the utilization of the press to provoke responses from other groups concerns Representative Adam Clayton Powell, who has utilized the opposition of the white press to build support in the black community. The desire of the white press to exclude Powell from Congress in the early 1960's and unfavorable news reports of his behavior only created more black support for him than had previously existed.

Dissuasion

A third symbolic strategy is dissuasion. This involves the utilization of symbols to discourage supporters of the other side from ac-

[12] "Study Finds No Negro 'Guerrillas,' " *Washington Post,* March 9, 1969, p. A9.
[13] *Ibid.*
[14] *Ibid.*

tive opposition and to encourage them to switch sides. This strategy is likely to be utilized in conjunction with arousal or in response to an opponent who is too successful at arousal. The most common example of this ploy is sending known personalities and entertainment figures to ghettos during the summer to "keep the lid on." Such stars discourage joining the militants and encourage constructive activities as an alternate to violence.

Another form of dissuasion is to discredit the cause of an opponent by linking it with some distasteful symbol. Symbols like *outside agitators, Communist inspired,* and *subversives* have been utilized to keep black residents out of the civil rights movement in a community. Similarly, civil rights leaders have branded their opposition as *racists* and *rednecks.* They use these terms to make the supporters of the opposing side reconsider their position and perhaps abandon it altogether.

When a group uses dissuasion, the larger the scope of the conflict, the greater the group's reliance on the press. For example, the mass media played a major role in publicizing the participation of entertainment figures in ghetto programs. Issue leaders are more dependent on the media for success in dissuasion than for success in arousal, because dissuasion will be utilized only when there is a degree of arousal, which may or may not have been achieved via the media.

Demonstration of Strength of Commitment

A fourth symbolic strategy is demonstration of strength of commitment. A characteristic of this tactic is that it is never used until all the others have failed or have been exhausted. In the civil rights movement, for example, all the other techniques were used to achieve some tangible rewards. When such strategies ceased to hold promise, a march on Washington was organized to demonstrate the strength and solidarity of the movement to governmental officials and the general public.

Other examples of such "last resort" shows of strength or commitment are the Jehovah's Witnesses' refusal to salute the flag; the black power sign given by some black American athletes at the Olympic Games at Mexico City in the summer of 1968; flag burnings at public rallies, and draft card burnings outside induction centers. The primary objective is to demonstrate the strength of commitment of a particular group and the size of the group that is making the commitment. An ancillary purpose may be to cause disruption, the cost of which is greater than some minimal type of concession.

Media receptivity is the highest for this strategy. Sheer numbers are often utilized to dramatize a grievance, creating the air of a spectacle. Another reason for media involvement is that this strategy usually marks a make-or-break point for the group. Failure of a show of strength can often mean public ridicule and a subsequent inability to mobilize support. For example, the civil rights movement was revitalized by the march on Washington in 1963, but the draft card burners lost all hope of public support when they resorted to public violations of the law.

Affirmation

The fifth type of symbolic strategy is affirmation. This strategy has no external function other than to revitalize group membership or to prod supporters to greater vigor in pressing the group's demands. Symbols used will stress *unity* and *solidarity*. Ordinarily there are two objectives of symbol dispensation: (1) to reinforce the adherents who have been associated with the cause from the outset; and (2) to reinforce the satellite groups, or those who joined the movement as a consequence of an appeal for support.

Affirmation can take a variety of forms. One is reference to physical fatigue of the leaders arising from their zealous activities to achieve group objectives. Another is reassurance of steadfastness of commitment. Albert Shanker constantly made this symbolic gesture to his teacher constituency during the New York school strike negotiations to quell rumors that the teachers were "being sold out." Another form is reference to the tenacity of the group. An example of such a reference is the phrase *we shall overcome,* which is utilized by the leaders of many causes, although it was civil rights groups who originally popularized the phrase. Finally, there are ritualized symbols that are used to foster a sense of group solidarity (for example, the V-for-peace sign, the flaming cross, and the clenched fist).

The mass media are relevant to group reinforcement at certain points in the group's development. The media becomes particularly important when the scope of the group's involvement increases to the extent that members can no longer receive leader reinforcement but must be reinforced in an impersonalized way. Most large groups have their own means of communication, such as a newspaper whose primary responsibility is to buoy the spirits of the followers. Union publications and ethnic papers are examples of such "cheerleading" publications.

Conclusion

The focus of this chapter has been on certain types of strategies that are utilized by groups to promote their causes. The key to success in each case is to put the appeal in a symbolic context that will have a maximum impact on followers, potential supporters, the opposition, or the decision-makers. Each strategy is dependent to some extent on the amount of attention that is provided by the mass media. Symbolic crusades, regardless of their form, are dependent on publicity so as to attract additional people or to give credibility to an issue commitment. Symbols and the media are two key mechanisms by which groups can channel their demands to a wider constituency and enhance their chances of success.

The next question that must be broached is, By what channels can an issue proceed from the systemic agenda of public controversy to the formal agenda? One means of finding the answer is to focus on the size of the public to which an issue can be expanded. It is the contention of the next chapter that the size of the audience can determine the means by which an issue will attain a formal agenda.

10

Entrance Patterns
and Agenda Access

In the past two chapters, we enumerated a series of propositions that linked the characteristics of an issue and its symbols to determine the likelihood of issue expansion. In this chapter, we focus on the various channels by which demands can be crystallized into formal agenda items. Each issue is likely to pass through defined channels to gain a place on the public docket, depending on the extent to which the issue has been enlarged.

We are hypothesizing that channels must be added to issue characteristics and symbols to gain an accurate picture of how an issue is transformed into a formal agenda item. This is summarized in the following diagram:

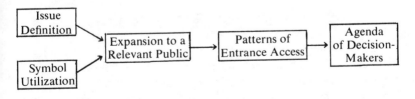

Before giving a series of propositions, a number of clarifying comments are in order. The previous chapters were concerned solely with aggregating demands and creating the systemic agenda; this chapter focuses on the consequences of a given degree of demand articulation. Access to a formal docket is a dynamic process, and our effort will be directed toward identifying the most common ways to translate demands into recognized problems facing decision-makers.

What specifically is involved in the problem of *agenda entrance?* The governmental agenda is concerned with the list of issues that a group of decision-makers at a given level of government identify as problems they must confront. What is the realm of issues that require some type of action? Having a place on the formal agenda does not necessarily mean that action will be taken. Often, actions will be deliberately delayed. All that is required for formal agenda status is that the leaders know that there is a problem that requires governmental action and make some type of response, even if it is only official recognition of the problem. There is no presumption that either of the contending parties in a dispute will be pleased with the ensuing action that a decisional unit will take once it gains the docket.

This chapter is based on two propositions. First, *the extent to which an issue is expanded will determine the means by which it achieves recognition.* By specifying the extent to which an issue has been enlarged to the four publics discussed earlier, we can determine the probable route by which an issue will attain recognition from governmental officials. Second, *the larger the public to which an issue has been expanded, the greater the likelihood of the conflict being placed on the docket.* Issues that are limited to the initial disputants are going to have greater difficulty attaining the attention of the decision-makers than disputes that have attained mass visibility. It will be recalled that the four types of publics include identification groups, attention groups, the attentive public, and the mass public.

Issues Confined to Identification Groups

When a conflict cannot be expanded beyond identification groups, it is likely to face great difficulty in gaining the attention of officials, who are already mired down in a welter of problems. In such a situation, groups must escalate their strategies to draw attention to their demands.

When conflicts are confined to identification groups, formal

agenda status is most likely to be attained only when disputants
threaten to disrupt the system. If groups have not attained positions
of strength within the system, they have no bargaining base other
than force or the threat of force. Thus, minority groups who cannot
involve others may resort to disruptive threats in order to force decision-makers to consider their demands. For example, the Black
Panthers "lose in public relations with a largely hostile or fearful
white community, . . . [but] gain in the kind of 'scare value' that
can wrest concessions from the . . . establishment." [1]

Often the threat of disruption is enough to create credibility.
Frequent acts of violence are unnecessary. Consider the case of the
Newark Black Panthers who openly espouse the trappings of vio-
lence, but produce few behavioral manifestations of it. As Ross
Baker noted:

> The black beret, the leather jacket and the clenched fist salute all
> point to a cohesive band of black insurgents bent on the destruc-
> tion of the system. The actual record of the Panthers indicates oth-
> erwise. There has not been a single violent incident . . . that has
> stemmed exclusively from Panther initiative.[2]

Sometimes, groups must reinforce threats with sporadic violent
outbursts to impress officials with their credibility. Groups that have
adopted this tactic include the Ku Klux Klan, the National Farmers
Union and the anti-war groups. Threats serve not only external goals,
but internal needs as well. As Lipsky writes, "Protest leaders have a
stake in perpetuating the notion that relatively powerless groups retain political efficacy despite what in many cases is obvious evidence
to the contrary." [3]

In some instances, the threat of force will cause a demand to be
placed on the agenda, but the response from the system will be totally antithetical to the demand. Groups resorting to violence face the
danger of being considered "subversive" or "agitators." In such a situation, their demands will not be met, and their actions will aid their
opponents. For example, consider the public outcry against the dem-

---

[1] Ross Baker, "A New Breed of Panther," *Washington Post,* March 2, 1969,
p. B2.
[2] *Ibid.*
[3] Michael Lipsky, "Protest as Political Resource," *American Political Science
Review* 62 (1968), p. 1154.

onstrators following the police incidents in Chicago during the Democratic National Convention in 1968. Threat has no guarantee of success, but we hypothesize that it will be used in the absence of other resources. As Lipsky has written, "Protest groups may well be able to raise the saliency of issues on the civic agenda through utilization of . . . threats to wider publics." [4]

Often when a group is newly arrived on the political scene, threats of violence and subsequent disruptive actions are its only means of communicating demands to the government. The communication initially will serve an educational function for the decision-makers, forcing them to become aware of the group, its aims, and its organizational structure. The substantive nature of their demands will become important only after the initial socialization. This procedure is in part what the Federal Alliance of Land Grants has attempted in New Mexico. The group is composed of a number of persons of Mexican heritage who claim on the basis of old Spanish land grants that a part of New Mexico belongs to them. Acts of violence have been initiated to force the relevant officials to learn more about the movement, as well as assay the relevance of their demands. But one observer notes:

> The ignorance of governmental officials of the basic nature of the movement is almost monumental. They tend to explain the Alianza away by easy, modern clichés. Some find in the references to common lands the spore of modern communism. [5]

Issues Confined to Attention Groups

Another channel is likely to be utilized by groups who are able to expand an issue to attention groups, but not further. In this instance, groups still resort to threats, but threats of a different nature. Their support is wide enough so that they do not have to resort to disruptive acts of violence. Nonetheless, they must make the decision-maker aware of their strength concerning an issue. The hypothesis is

---

[4] *Ibid.*

[5] Joseph Love, "La Raza: Mexican-Americans in Rebellion," *Transaction* 6, No. 4 (February, 1969), p. 39.

that *conflicts that are confined to attention publics are most likely to be brought to the agenda by threats of imminent sanctions.*

Anthony Downs has written that in an effort to obtain his own best interest, an individual will organize with others to obtain certain desired benefits from government. If these benefits are not forthcoming, then the optimal strategy is to threaten to withhold votes at the upcoming election. If the voting bloc has been loyal in the past and is likely to vote in sufficient numbers to sway the outcome, then the decision-makers are wont to reconsider their positions. Downs identifies the ballot box as a primary sanction, which may take the form of either voting for the opposition or abstaining. He characterizes individuals who threaten sanctions as "favor-buyers."

> They [favor-buyers] are men who wish a party to act in some way which benefits them, and will in return influence voters to support that party. Favor-buyers claim to represent no one except themselves; they are merely engaged in trading their influence over voters for specific acts they want done.[6]

The threat to withhold support at an election can become a pivotal bargaining ploy. Many groups have used this method in an effort to gain access to the agenda. In recent campaigns, black leaders have attempted to speak for millions of potential voters in order to gain some type of concessions. In addition, threats can be made for other types of sanctions, such as withholding money from campaign coffers while still voting for the party, or minimizing efforts for a particular set of candidates.

These types of sanctions are not extralegal and may be distinguished from disruption. The effectiveness of the threat depends on the size of the group, its solidarity, the amount of support it has given decision-makers in the past, the closeness of the election, etc.

Issues Confined to the Attentive Public

Occasionally, a dispute goes beyond the purview of a coalition of various interest groups to reach the attentive public. When a group is

[6] Anthony Downs, *An Economic Theory of Democracy* (New York: Harper, 1957), p. 88.

able to secure the attention of those who keep informed about an issue or a variety of issues, then its resource base is widened, and the group has a firm position for confronting decision-makers with a particular issue. The proposition is: *conflicts that are confined to the attentive public are likely to attain the formal agenda through a brokerage channel.*

Conflicts that have reached the stratum of well-informed people are largely systemic agenda items such as public housing, pollution, welfare benefits, and specific tax policies. In such instances, conflicting parties use intermediaries, such as political parties, to place their demands on the agenda. Groups must go through a prolonged process of lining up support from a wide stratum of attentive people so that the level of concern is broad enough to force decision-makers to make some type of response, even if they merely consider the problem superficially.

The pollution problem attained formal agenda standing in this manner. Widespread public apathy about water and air purification led interested groups to band together and disseminate information to the public concerning the possible dangers if certain policies continued. Ultimately, with the mass media's help in publicizing dangers in urban areas, the issue attained systemic agenda status and was subsequently transformed into a governmental agenda item.

Often, a group must turn an issue into a symbolic crusade to attract the support necessary to gain a bargaining position with political parties. For example, aid to public and parochial schools was an explosive issue that had been raised unsuccessfully many times. However, Catholic leaders such as Cardinal Francis Spellman were finally able to place the issue on the agenda by referring to proposals that were "fair and equitable to all students." [7] The issue became so salient that the parties had to confront the issue and attempt to translate it into some type of policy solution. Legislators are sensitive to issues that attract sizable attention. But as Hugh Price notes:

> Every Congressional session involves hundreds of little legislative skirmishes, only a few of which develop into full scale battles. . . .

[7] Hugh Douglas Price, "Race, Religion and Congressmen: The Kennedy Aid to Education Program," in Alan Westin (ed.), *The Centers of Power: 3 Cases in American National Government* (New York: Harcourt, 1964), p. 38.

> Such temperature issues as . . . the role of parochial schools are
> generally beyond the ability of Congress to handle.[8]

As a consequence, such issues may become a permanent part of the
formal agenda, appearing at recurring intervals but never being fully
resolved.

Issues Expanded to the Mass Public

In a few instances, the mass public becomes involved with an issue.
Then, the response from the system is almost reflexive; decision-makers
automatically place the issue on the governmental agenda. Once
such issues are included in the list of items confronting policy-makers,
they will remain up for reconsideration until they are resolved or
until times require their redefinition or reappraisal.

An example of mass-involvement occurred early in 1969. An
offshore well operated by the Union Oil Company sprang a leak, and
the resulting oil slick began destroying wildlife and miles of California
beach. As a consequence, many enraged citizens formed an organization
called GOO (get oil out). They collected over 50,000 signatures
in three days on a petition calling for the President to stop
subsea coastal oil drilling. Almost immediately, the government announced
that these operations were to be temporarily halted pending
a thorough review. The alacrity of the decision-makers' response
demonstrates elite concern with a mass issue.[9]

Other examples of mass issues include work stoppages involving
the automobile workers and steel workers and public employees such
as members of the transit union, firemen, police, and teachers; the
gun control issue that was raised after the assassination of President
Kennedy; and foreign threats, such as the presence of missiles in
Cuba in 1963.

Such an issue does not start as a dispute, then develop into a
conflict that gradually expands to the mass public through a series of
redefinitions. Its translation to the mass public is immediate, as is its
spot on the governmental agenda.

[8] *Ibid.,* pp. 69–70.
[9] Kimmis Hendrick, "Santa Barbarans Gird to Prevent Future Oil Pollution,"
Christian Science Monitor, February 19, 1969, p. 6.

Durability of the Issue

Once an issue gains formal agenda standing, what can be said of its life expectancy? How long will it remain? Most issues, upon gaining a position on the docket, have a "built-in life" that assures their existence over a number of years regardless of how they are resolved. Even if the issue is "solved," there is continuous debate over how the program is going to be administered, who is going to be serviced, etc. For example, social security ceased to be an issue after its adoption in the 1930's, but it remained on the governmental agenda because its coverage was disputed.

Since issues are seldom removed from the docket once they gain access, what implications does this have for new issues that are developing? First, there is a saturation problem for the system. So many old issues are always guaranteed a spot on the docket, new disputes must gain a considerable amount of attention before they will be considered. Second, one of the easiest ways of attaining access is by defining an issue in terms of one of the items already on the agenda. The Medicare issue, for example, was always broached by its supporters as a necessary extension of the Social Security program, a well-established policy that would require minimal adjustment with the adoption of Medicare.

Once an issue is resolved in the sense that the problem will no longer be considered, it can often provide a precedent by which future disputes can be resolved. For example, supporters say that American recognition of the diplomatic status of Mainland China would not imply approval of the country's policies, since the United States has recognized the Soviet Union, Latin American dictatorships, and even Nazi Germany.

Conclusion

Thus, the channel by which an issue is brought before decision-makers depends on the extent to which a conflict is made visible to various publics. The wider the audience, the greater the chance that the dispute will reach the docket of problems confronting decision-makers. Once an issue attains the formal agenda, it is unlikely that the issue will be removed from the docket itself. Even if it is removed, one of its by-products may be a hangover demanding system attention for some years to come.

11

Toward a Theory of Agenda-Building

This volume has dealt with the dynamics of how the expansion of issues to larger publics acts as a prelude to formal agenda consideration. A model has been advanced to demonstrate a network that produces salient issues requiring consideration by decision-makers. Consideration has been given to the way an issue is defined, the nature of the language used by the leadership of involved groups, and the channels through which an issue may go to attain agenda status.

Issues arise from group conflict. These issues may eventually command a position on the agenda of governmental decision-makers, who manage group conflict. An important way in which an issue may gain access to a governmental agenda is by expanding in scope, intensity, and visibility. These processes are important determinants of where the conflicts will be resolved and how the issues will ultimately be defined, so groups attempt to control them to promote their own interests.

Two types of agendas have been identified. The first, the systemic agenda of controversy, consists of the full range of issues or problem areas that are both salient to a political community and commonly perceived as legitimate subjects of governmental concern. The systemic agenda is not in any sense a formal agenda. It exists only in the sense that popular concerns, priorities, and values will both prescribe and proscribe the type of questions upon which authoritative decisions may be rendered. The systemic agenda is formed through the normal struggle of social forces. At any point in time, it will reflect the existing balance of these forces, or the "mobilization of bias" within a community.

The second type of agenda is much more formal and represents those items explicitly scheduled for the active and serious consideration of a decision-making unit. We have referred to this type of agenda as an institutional or governmental agenda. Every governmental unit, be it local, state, or national, will have such an agenda. Some items on these agendas will overlap, but each agenda will have items that are intrinsic exclusively to it. Decision-makers may take action to alleviate a grievance on the agenda or decide to take no action.

Thus, formal agenda status does not necessarily imply remedial or corrective action; it simply means that decision-makers will officially recognize and consider a matter. Often a problem will appear on a formal agenda some years before corrective action is taken. This is particularly true when the issue is salient to a great number of people but is not sufficiently urgent to overcome the objections of an entrenched, vocal minority or to justify the potential disruption that its resolution might create. For example, the question of Medicare for the aged was on the formal agenda for decades before decision-makers adopted a corrective program.

In general, it has been our contention that perhaps the surest way for an issue to attain and maintain formal agenda standing is first through entry onto the systemic agenda of controversy. While it is possible for an item to attain access to a formal agenda without having gained systemic agenda standing, it is unlikely that any issue of major social consequences will become a formal agenda item without prior standing on the systemic agenda.

In determining which set of issues out of a muddle of confusing, conflicting disputes will attain the public docket, we posited that a cluster of characteristics relating to an issue is critical in determining the likelihood of its success. To reach the formal agenda, an issue should evoke a response on the mass level, since visibility helps a dispute gain the attention of political decision-makers. To attain such a position of public recognition, the issue should be defined or redefined (if the initial definition fails to bring a public response) as ambiguously as possible, with implications for as many people as possible, involving issues other than the dispute in question, with no categorical precedence, and as simply as is feasible.

In expanding a dispute, other elements come into play. The symbols, or language, in which the issue is phrased will often bear on the range of possible onlookers who become cognizant of the controversy. This, in turn, will affect the type of symbolic manipulation that is possible and the receptivity of the mass media, both of which influence the ultimate scope of the conflict. The channels by which issues reach governmental agendas will depend on the size of the mass that is exposed to, and identifies with, the dispute.

In the enumeration of these various factors, analysis has been confined to case studies. Future studies might use these as indicators for formulating more rigorous tests of the propositions we have advanced.

Implications for Democratic Theory

At the outset of this study, it was suggested that the processes of agenda-building were a critical, but largely unexamined, facet of democratic politics. What implications does this newly identified dimension of political behavior hold for democratic theory? There are at least three important implications that go to the very heart of modern democratic thought. They center on (1) the social precursors of democratic rule, (2) the nature of popular participation, and (3) the prospects for social change. These implications serve not so much to refute existing theory as to extend and elaborate on it.

SOCIAL PRECURSORS OF DEMOCRATIC RULE. Modern theory correctly recognizes that the stability of a democratic system depends heavily on the social context in which it operates. Thus, modern theory typically emphasizes the importance of social pluralism, which serves at least two vital functions. First, it allows for the operation of an almost laissez-faire type of system of social checks and balances that tends to prevent any single group or interest from totally dominating the system. Second, through overlapping group memberships and cross-cutting solidarities, social pluralism acts to mitigate the intensity of conflict and to prevent the superimposition of one conflict upon another.

Note that these social precursors are seen primarily as providing a setting in which democratic government may operate—a setting that promotes the stability of the overall system. Stability is of paramount importance, and attention is focused upon social *conditions* but not on the social *processes* that impinge upon and determine the concerns of political decision-makers. Moreover, modern theory tends to overlook the inherent bias that will be present in any system and does little to explain how this bias developed and how it might be changed. Further, by taking the setting as a given, it posits an essentially static social environment and tends to ignore the mutual interdependence of social and political processes. The agenda-building perspective, however, alerts us to the importance of pre-decisional social processes in determining what occurs at the decisional stage and the types of policy outcomes that will be produced. These processes are very much related to the question of bias in the system and the range of issues that will be considered legitimate items of public controversy. The agenda-building perspective further assumes an inextricable and mutually interdependent relationship between the concerns generated in the social environment and the vitality of the governmental process.

POPULAR PARTICIPATION. Modern theory has correctly noted that direct participation in the decision-making of a large-scale democracy is necessarily limited. Nonetheless, modern theory insists upon the importance of providing the opportunity for widespread mass involvement at recurrent intervals. As Dahl has noted, "The election is the critical technique for insuring that governmental leaders will be relatively responsive to non-leaders." [1]

The agenda-building perspective, however, suggests that the importance of popular participation may go well beyond simply voting or participating in the selection of political leaders. It emphasizes the crucial role that various publics may play in shaping the very substance of governmental decisions. It, thus, reopens what Litt has called "a fundamental, although ancient, question of political analy-

[1] Robert Dahl, *A Preface to Democratic Theory* (Chicago: The University of Chicago Press, 1956), p. 125.

sis, namely, the extent to which politics is merely a device for determining the composition of the governing entity and the extent to which it is a device for evolving new and durable mechanisms for distributing more fully the social goods of a society." [2]

By its very nature, participation in the agenda-building process is open and widespread. Such involvement may be more important to the long run stability of the system than electoral participation. While elections may fortify the short-term stability of a system, this will go for naught if the content of formal agendas does not reflect the substance of the systemic agenda, or is not responsive to changes in that agenda. As Litt notes,

> The failure of the policy elites to channel participation into creative institutions producing more social valuables in tax, welfare, and employment policies will produce the violent outbursts that undermine polity and the aspirations of its disadvantaged members.[3]

Thus, modern democratic theory suggests minimal popular participation, while the agenda-building framework makes allowances for continuing mass involvement. In the latter, passive acceptance of the status quo is a critical input, fortifying the existing mobilization of bias and limiting the development and formulation of public policy issues. Further, mass participation may be one of the major innovative forces in developing new issues and refining old issues that have remained on the formal agenda for some time. In sum, the agenda-building perspective serves to broaden the range of recognized influences on the public policy-making process.

SOCIAL CHANGE.   Modern democratic theory tends to portray a politics of accommodation that permits incremental response to new demands and slow but ordered social change. As Litt notes: "the essence of accommodation politics . . . [is] an underlying consensus on the enduring stability of pluralistic politics. . . . [It is] a slack system designed to produce selective change within a seemingly stable social order." [4] Problems are dealt with in a piecemeal fashion, and changes never depart markedly from the status quo. Modern

[2] Edgar Litt, *Beyond Pluralism: Ethnic Politics in America* (Glenview, Illinois: Scott, Foresman and Company, 1970), p. 153.
[3] *Ibid.*, p. 154.
[4] *Ibid.*, p. 157.

theory says little about the prospects for major social innovation within a democratic framework. It scarcely acknowledges the possibility of major social movements developing "to break society's logjams, to prevent ossification in the political system, to prompt and justify major innovations in social policy and economic organization." [5]

On the other hand, an agenda-building framework allows us to begin to cope more effectively with the problems of social change and does not presume that the status quo is the necessary basis or point of departure for all social change. It helps provide an understanding of why major change normally occurs only under conditions of widespread popular mobilization, or "crisis politics." For example, from the agenda-building perspective, it is easy to understand how and why "the riots of the past few summers have caused individual local crises and have collectively led to a sense of national crisis, triggering a concern about the accommodation and political style of urban Negroes. . . . Negro demands, although often blocked on the local level, are rechanneled, through leadership and the creation of crises, to the national level." [6] In illuminating these processes, the agenda-building paradigm offers preliminary answers to why some issues make a formal agenda while others do not, even though their merits may be the same.

Implications for Practical Politics

By ignoring the agenda-building process, modern theory may inadvertently foster the view that democratic politics is more static than it need be. This may contribute to despair, frustration, and anger on the part of those who have no apparent recourse for ameliorating their grievances or demands. Lacking formal influence or access to the centers of governmental authority, dissonant elements may resort to anomic behavior ranging from total withdrawal to violent displays of rage. Although such anomic action may promote general societal awareness of the grievance, it can be counter-productive from an agenda-building point of view and hamper the mobilization of bias

[5] Jack Walker, "A Critique of the Elitist Theory of Democracy," *American Political Science Review* 60 (1966), p. 294.
[6] Litt, *op. cit.*, pp. 105–6.

necessary to achieve systemic agenda status. For example, the willingness expressed by groups such as the Black Panthers to embrace violence to further their objectives has probably promoted greater repression and alienated considerable potential support among both blacks and whites.

If a democratic system is to survive and major changes are to occur short of fullscale revolution, the principal forces for change must participate in shaping the agenda of legitimate controversy. Once a grievance reaches this systemic agenda, formal governmental agenda consideration is likely, if not inevitable. This is not to say that the process will necessarily be rapid. Even the most urgent grievances may linger for years before ameliorative action is forthcoming. The wheels of democracy grind slowly but can be accelerated through popular mobilization.

To participate effectively in the agenda-building process, a group must first be organized. That is the simple lesson that people like Saul Alinsky have tried to teach. However, as contemporary groups have learned, organization is not enough. To elevate a demand to systemic agenda standing, a group needs both organization and effective strategy attuned to the processes we have described. Many of the propositions developed here point directly to such strategies.

In fact, most of the ploys discussed previously have been used by persons and groups to their advantage quite unconsciously or with little understanding of how and why they work. In many instances, our propositions represent little more than explicit articulation of what to the experienced politician amounts to "political intuition" or "savvy."

All of this is not to say that violence and extralegal actions will necessarily be ineffective or dysfunctional. A dramatic or startling incident may be required to gain popular recognition or to assure attention for a grievance. While we are inclined to agree with H. L. Nieburg who asserts that all acts of violence are potentially functional,[7] it must be noted that this does not necessarily mean that violence will be functional to its perpetrators. Unless it can be skillfully exploited, violence is likely to be turned to the advantage of the op-

[7] H. L. Nieburg, "The Threat of Violence and Social Change," *American Political Science Review* 56 (1962), p. 867.

position and used to cloud, if not deny, the legitimacy of actual grievances.

Alternative Approaches to the Study of Agenda-Building

While this study has concentrated exclusively on the problems of agenda-building in the American political setting, the propositions we have advanced refer to general social processes that may be subject to study in other political systems. Comparative studies from the agenda-building point of view might reveal important, previously unidentified or unexamined similarities and differences in the processes that generally characterize political systems. For example, To what extent does the number of access points in a political system influence the likelihood that conflicts will reach the governmental agenda through legitimate channels?

In the American context, traditional analyses of case study materials can be more useful if pursued within some theoretical framework. The framework provided here can serve as one possible perspective for examining an issue conflict. A variety of such case studies would provide a data base for evaluating the theoretical propositions advanced in the text. However, the study of agenda-building requires more than careful analysis of issue conflicts. The attitudes and beliefs of the participants are conditioned by events antecedent to the particular issue involved. The question then arises of how people acquire their orientations toward symbols, personalities, etc., which are manipulated by protagonists in an issue conflict.

Perhaps, a prerequisite to this type of analysis would be the study of the distribution of symbolic meaning (that is, the specific content of symbols) among both specific and general publics. That would enable analysts to map various patterns of symbolic attachments in the populace and relate them to specific issue conflicts. Subcultures of symbolic meaning may exist that are behaviorally more important in explaining the dynamics of issue conflicts than ethnicity, social class, status, region, or other traditional modes of differentiating social groups or cleavage lines.

Another aspect of the problem that remains to be explored is a more complete conceptualization of how issues gain attention through extralegal or nonlegitimate means. The primary focus of this book has been processes that fall largely within the bounds of accepted system norms. However, violence, protest, and mass movements are also vehicles of agenda-building that should be subjected to more thorough scrutiny.

A Two-Way Channel

This book has focused on delineating the steps by which a dispute becomes a formal agenda item. Except for a broad enumeration of some of the strategies that public officials might use to contain conflicts, very little attention has been paid to the problem of what happens after the issue is placed on a formal agenda. While the decision-making process is fairly well understood, what happens after decisions are made? The major aspects of the post-decisional phase need to be delineated more fully to show how decisions are transformed into action programs.

In achieving this aim, a number of distinctions may be relevant. The distinction between symbolic and tangible rewards is at the crux of the post-decisional problem of resource allocation.[8] One might focus on how different types of rewards are distributed in different situations. Special attention should be given to how language and issue characteristics are manipulated by officials to achieve certain desired outcomes.

Another relevant dimension in outcome analysis is that of social control. As Gamson writes:

> Any political system must handle discontented groups in some fashion. . . . One response attempts to remove pressure from dissidents by yielding ground (i.e., outcome modification), the other by directing counter-influences or social control. Social control will generally be preferred . . . since . . . it will maximize the maneuverability of the recipient of pressure.[9]

The alternatives for social control available to any decisional unit are varied. The type of control mechanism will depend on the

[8] Murray Edelman, *The Symbolic Uses of Politics* (Urbana: University of Illinois Press, 1964), p. 22.
[9] William Gamson, "Stable Unrepresentation in American Society," *American Behavioral Scientist* 12 (1968), pp. 18–19.

type of issue involved and on how many people are directly involved. To understand the nature of social control, it is therefore important to delineate the types of techniques that permit "stability to be achieved for considerable periods of time during which substantial unmet needs are present among many members of the society." [10]

Temporal Change

Another aspect of the outcome problem relates to time. Immediate consequences of resource allocation may be different from the long-run implications of the resolution of a particular issue.

For example, the ultimate resolution of the maelstrom of problems associated with racial conflict may depend in part on the acquisition of skills by people who matured in the late 1950's when the problem first became visible. Studies on black-white attitudes indicate a considerable discrepancy in outlooks between the two races regarding ameliorative solutions to problems of integrated housing and the like. Thus, any policy solution in the short run may be viewed solely in terms of immediate needs, but the long run consequences may urge combatants to bide time until another generation assumes a greater share of political responsibility in program definition and maintenance. [11]

Postscript

In conclusion, it may be appropriate to address ourselves to the question of the relevance of the study of agenda-building. As was suggested at the outset, agenda-building affords a perspective on political processes that both allows and demands that one draw upon a number of salient approaches to the study of politics. It thus provides a framework for integrating existing knowledge and guiding future research. However, the relevance of the study of agenda-building ex-

[10] *Ibid.*, p. 19.
[11] Angus Campbell and Howard Schumann, "Racial Attitudes in Fifteen American Cities," in *Supplemental Studies for the National Advisory Commission on Civil Disorders* (Washington, D.C.: United States Government Printing Office, 1968), pp. 34–37.

Epilogue

Agenda-building is an integral part of the public policy-making process. Throughout this volume, we have emphasized the importance of agenda-building in structuring the more substantive transactions of politics. We have also stressed the variable nature of the agenda-building process, its potential fluidity, and the opportunities it affords for popular involvement. In this final chapter, we would like to elaborate on these themes and to share some reflections on the constantly changing context of agenda-building in the United States.

Agenda-Building and the Stakes of Politics

The social and political significance of agenda-building arises in part from the fact that it serves to structure subsequent policy choices. However, the stakes involved do not reside solely in the prospects of future policies. There are more immediate payoffs involved. These take the form of social recognition and the validation of certain values, interests, and beliefs to the exclusion of others. These payoffs are determined by the issues and issue definitions that ultimately command formal agenda standing and by the participants and views represented in the process.

Government is inevitably involved in the social allocation of prestige and in the social construction of reality. In fact, Edelman suggests that "government affects behavior chiefly by shaping the cognitions of large numbers of people in ambiguous situations. It helps to create their beliefs about what is proper; their perceptions of what is fact; and their expectations of what is to come."[1]

In giving an issue formal agenda status, government conveys important messages about who and what are socially important, about what is and is not problematic, and about what does and does not fall within the legitimate purview of government. Because these messages bear the imprimatur of public authority, they serve to define winners and losers in a social and political sense just as the more material allocations of government define them in an economic sense. As a consequence, claimants, as well as members of the general public, can find both personal satisfaction and social vindication in the mere fact of official recognition and consideration of their concerns.[2]

To appreciate the stakes in the agenda-building process it is necessary to recognize the indeterminate nature of most public policy problems. Policy problems are not simply "givens," nor are they simply matters of the "facts" of a situation. They are matters of interpretation and social definition. As Gusfield writes:

> Human problems do not spring up, full-blown and announced, into the consciousness of bystanders. Even to recognize a situation as painful requires a system for categorizing and defining events. All situations that are experienced as painful do not become matters of public activity and targets for public action. Neither are they given the same meaning at all times and by all peoples. "Objective" conditions are seldom so compelling and so clear in their form that they spontaneously generate a "true" consciousness.[3]

Policy problems are socially constructed. They arise not so much from events and circumstances as from the meanings that people

[1] Murray Edelman, *Politics as Symbolic Action* (Chicago: Markman, 1971), p. 7.
[2] See, for example, Mark Nadel, *The Politics of Consumer Protection* (Indianapolis: Bobbs-Merrill, 1971), p. 62; and Louis A. Zurcher and R. George Kirkpatrick, *Citizens for Decency* (Austin: University of Texas Press, 1976), pp. 218–19.
[3] Joseph Gusfield, *The Culture of Public Problems* (Chicago: University of Chicago Press, 1981), p. 3.

attribute to those events and circumstances. Whether or not a situation is considered a public problem and what the problem is, if there is one, depends upon not just facts but upon beliefs and values—beliefs and values that determine what is taken to be fact, what facts are considered relevant, and how those facts are interpreted. Thus,

> as ideas and consciousness public problems have a structure which involves both a cognitive and a moral dimension. The cognitive side consists in beliefs about the facticity of the situation and events comprising the problem—our theories and empirical beliefs about poverty, mental disorders, alcoholism, and so forth. The moral side is that which enables the situation to be viewed as painful, ignoble, or immoral. It is what makes alteration or eradication desirable or continuation valuable. The moral side of a problem suggests a condemnable state of affairs from the perspective of someone's morality.[4]

Because public problems are socially constructed, a multiplicity of definitions of the problem is always possible. At issue is not so much which definition is correct but which is most credible and politically acceptable at any particular time. This is not to say that all definitions are equally arbitrary. Some may be better grounded empirically and some may be potentially more useful than others. However, usefulness necessarily implies value judgments and even the most objective facts cannot establish what is desirable or resolve difficult value tradeoffs. Moreover, in the complex web of social life, *the* facts are almost always uncertain and subject to change in unanticipated ways. They are seldom so clear and abundant as to permit an unambiguous assessment of the problem. Of necessity then

> problems are man-made. There are always multiple conceptions. What, for instance, is *the* problem in health; too much or too little doctoring, the failure of individuals to follow healthy habits, or the failure of the medical system to deliver health services? Does *the* problem of education lie in the inability of some students to learn or in the incapacity of teachers to teach? . . . Actually, the objectives implied by answers to these questions, however one answers them, are all being pursued. The universal tendency for the grab bag of

4 Gusfield, *op. cit.*, p. 9.

objectives to be multiple, conflicting, and vague should be evidence enough that problems are not uniquely determined.[5]

To define a policy problem is to imply its solution and to delimit its solution possibilities. Situations defined as inevitable and unalterable, however lamentable, are not likely to be considered policy problems but rather just hard facts of life. Of course, such definitions change over time as what was once inconceivable becomes conceivable and vice versa.

The definition of a problem presupposes certain realities, and its solution or possible solutions are based on those presuppositions. Both the presuppositions and the solutions they may predicate are potentially matters of conflict and are subject to change over time. "Those committed to one or another solution of a problem see its genesis in the necessary consequences of events and processes; those in opposition often point to 'agitators' who impose one or another definition of reality." [6]

Consider, for example, the controversies that have raged over the past decade regarding the government's responsibilities to the handicapped. These controveries have centered in part on the issue of accessible public transportation for the handicapped. Those who define the problem as a matter of providing cost-efficient transportation suggest that the solution lies in distinct services specifically designed to meet the special needs of the handicapped and available exclusively to them. Thus, they point to things like taxi vouchers or specially equipped dial-a-ride vans. This definition and its implied solutions, however, are not only objectionable but odious to many advocates of the rights of handicappers. At issue, they argue, are equality of treatment and the integration of the handicapped as fully as possible into normal American life. Thus, to provide separate or distinct services for the handicapped not only misses the point but actually exacerbates the problem by further segregating the handicapped and treating them differently. What is needed, these advocates suggest, is a redesigning and modification of all public transportation facilities to make them fully accessible to the handicapped.

[5] Aaron Wildavsky, *Speaking Truth to Power: The Art and Craft of Policy Analysis* (Boston: Little, Brown, 1979), p. 57.
[6] Gusfield, *op. cit.*, p. 3.

Further examples of such definitional conflict are found in the contemporary controversies over the Equal Rights Amendment and abortion. At issue in both cases is not only the solution but just what the problem is or whether there even is a problem. Similar examples are found in the areas of environmental protection and energy development. In fact, such controversies abound and are what much of politics is about.

Because of their indeterminant nature, most policy problems are never really solved in any complete or definitive sense. Problems are worked on and perhaps transformed only to be superseded or displaced by new and more pressing ones. Changing events and circumstances can alter the facts or the balance of forces that sustain particular definitions of a problem. Changing values and beliefs can also prompt redefinitions as "what is desired itself continues to change under reconsideration." [7]

> Our words (hence our thoughts) imply that problems have solutions, as if they could be solved once and for all, but our experience suggests that, like the poor, they are always with us. It is our expectation of closure, . . . rather than regeneration and rebirth, . . . that is misleading. . . . Problems are defined by hypothetical solutions; the problem's formulation and the proposed solution are part of the same hypothesis. . . . Problems are not so much solved as superseded. [8]

That policy problems tend to be inherently ambiguous and are rarely solved in any final sense does not mean that they are unimportant or that efforts to cope with them, often through uneasy compromises, are without important consequences. It simply means choices must be made and that those choices begin with the definition of the problem in the agenda-building process. How the problem is defined has the effect of structuring subsequent choices by circumscribing its solution possibilities. To define the problem of highway safety, for example, as a problem of bad drivers points to a different set of possible solutions than if the problem is defined as one of unsafe cars, inadequate roads, lax law enforcement, or the lack of a balanced transportation system.

[7] Charles Lindblom, "The Science of 'Muddling Through,'" *Public Administration Review* 19 (1959), p. 86.
[8] Wildavsky, *op. cit.*, p. 83.

More immediately, how the problem is defined has the effect of allocating responsibility or blame; of rendering judgments on the comparative social worth of different groups and people; and of affirming or disapproving certain values, beliefs, and life styles. With such stakes, it is easy to see why conflict over the definition of an issue can be so intense and why the ability to control or influence that definition is so important not only in terms of subsequent policy actions, but also as an end in itself.

Problem Definition and Agenda Consequences

That policy problems are socially constructed and presuppose possible solutions has important agenda-building implications. Perhaps the most notable and obvious of these is that who participates, and how, can make a difference. It can make a difference in terms of what problems gain formal agenda access, how those problems are defined, and what relationship they bear to issues on the public or systemic agenda. However, regardless of who participates, unless the definition of a situation implies a plausible solution or the means to a solution, an issue is not likely to be treated as a policy problem nor accorded formal agenda standing. Demands that merely point to a situation about which "something should be done" may evoke sympathy and may even reach the public agenda, but without fuller definition they are unlikely to command more than *pro forma* attention from governmental decision-makers. As a consequence, gaps between the formal and the systemic agendas may arise simply from the absence of plausible solutions to commonly recognized but ill-defined problems.

To be plausible, of course, the solution possibilities implied by the definition of a policy problem must be feasible within the bounds of available resources and accepted values and beliefs; otherwise, they will be dismissed as fanciful, irrelevant, or even odious. Because plausibility rests in part on "conventional wisdom," the test of plausibility tends to inhibit innovative definitions or redefinitions of policy problems. Such definitions are likely to be accepted only when the conventional wisdom relating to the problem has been discredited or changed. In the United States, for example, because poverty has traditionally been conceived of as an individual-level problem, there is a reluctance to accept any definition suggesting structural- or systemic-level solutions.

Just as problems may be officially ignored for want of a solution, the emergence of a solution may make possible the recognition of a public policy problem. We normally think of policy problems as having their origins in events and circumstances. These create difficulties, which, in turn, prompt a search for solutions. Often, however, this is not the case. In the absence of readily available solutions, we simply accept or learn to live with many difficult situations. The impetus then for the definition (or redefinition) of a situation as a problem may come from the availability of a solution just waiting, if not actively searching, for a problem to "solve." As Cohen and March write: "A solution is somebody's product. A computer is not just a solution to a problem, . . . discovered when needed. It is an answer actively looking for a question. . . . Despite the dictum that you cannot find the answer until you have formulated the question well, you often do not know what the question is in . . . problem solving until you know the answer." [9]

A notable example is found in the contemporary issue of abortion. With the development of the technology that made abortion a relatively safe and inexpensive clinical procedure, it became something of a solution in search of a problem. It then became an issue because people strongly disagreed on what problem or problems, if any, it was an acceptable solution to. As this example suggests, changing knowledge and technological developments are likely to contribute to an expanding governmental agenda not so much because of the problems they create, but because of the problems they make possible. The same could be said of expanding resources.

Because policy problems are socially constructed, conflicting definitions of a particular problem are both possible and likely. Such conflicting definitions tend to be based on different conceptions of, or perspectives on, the realities of a situation. As a consequence, they tend to presuppose different, often contradictory, solutions. Consistency is, of course, a logical imperative, not a political one. Thus, the presence of mutually contradictory definitions does not preclude either or both from becoming active items on the governmental agenda nor from being acted upon as matters of public policy. A well-known example of this is found in the policies simultaneously pur-

[9] Michael Cohen and James March, *Leadership and Ambiguity: The American College President* (New York: McGraw-Hill, 1974), p. 82.

sued by the federal government to discourage the smoking of tobacco while supporting its production. Governmental acceptance of logically inconsistent definitions of, and solutions to, policy problems is facilitated by the disjointed nature and fragmented structure of the American policy process. As long as they can be treated in mutual isolation, either in time or through different institutional processes, inconsistent definitions of a problem cannot only be handled by the political system but can simultaneously serve as bases for public policies.

It is only when conflicting definitions come into direct confrontation with one another that they become politically incompatible. Such conflicts over the definition of a problem create uncertainties that policy-makers are likely to avoid. As a consequence, problems that involve competing definitions are not likely to be accorded formal agenda status unless the mobilization of bias is distinctly one-sided in both scope and intensity. If the problem is broadly salient, this condition is most likely to obtain only in the face of a recognized crisis or scandal. Of course, whether a particular situation constitutes a crisis or scandal as opposed to being merely a dramatic event or a regrettable set of circumstances is itself a matter of definition.

The impetus of events is important but what ultimately counts is the interpretation given to them. Annually, for example, Americans murder or maim one another with firearms at a rate that would surely be considered scandalous in most countries of the world. However, proponents of gun control have not generally been successful in tipping the mobilization of bias sufficiently to sustain a definition of the problem as one of effective gun control. In the absence of an effectively exploited event or a galvanizing set of circumstances, policy-makers will be reluctant to confront the issue. Thus, the issue is likely to go unattended and the gap between the formal and systemic agendas is likely to be exacerbated. Such has been the fate of gun control in the United States.

While different definitions of policy problems tend to point to different solution possibilities, the solution possibilities implied by the definitions of seemingly unrelated problems can overlap. As a consequence, people may agree on a solution without agreeing on what it is a solution to. Convergence on a solution without prior agreement on the focal problem is fairly common in legislative decision-making. The food stamp program enacted in 1964, for example, won initial support from legislators who saw it as a solution to the problems of stabilizing farm prices and promoting agriculture as well as from legislators primarily concerned with the problems of hunger and helping the poor.

Both problem definitions and solutions that have previously won acceptance on the governmental agenda are prime candidates for use in defining new problems or redefining old ones so as to gain agenda standing. For many years prior to 1965, for example, educators had unsuccessfully advocated federal aid as a solution to the problem of local school finance. However, that idea won a more or less permanent position on the federal agenda in 1965 only after it was redefined as a partial solution to the problem of poverty, a problem definition that had been legitimized by previous policies promoted by Lyndon Johnson as part of his War on Poverty.[10] Similarly in the 1970's, deregulation and deinstitutionalization, once legitimized, became general purpose palliatives linked to all manner of problems.

Participation in the Agenda-Building Process

The right to participate in determining what issues the government will address and how they are defined is an important stake in the agenda-building process. Nominally, this right is widely distributed; and this fact itself serves as an important constraint on policy-makers. Insensitivity to this general right invites popular repudiation not only of offending policy-makers but also of the process and its product. Nonetheless, the fact remains that control over the governmental agenda is ultimately in the hands of office holders, and active participation in the processes through which it is formulated tends to be rather narrowly circumscribed. Moreover, as we have previously noted, this participation tends to be distinctly biased in favor of some groups and issues and not others. "The public arena is not a field on which all play on equal terms; some have greater access than others and greater power and ability to shape the definition of public issues." [11]

In general, the governmental agenda will tend to reflect the problems and priorities that are salient to those most actively involved

[10] See, for example, Jerome Murphy, "The Education Bureaucracies Implement Novel Policy," in Allan P. Sindler (ed.), *Policy and Politics in America: Six Case Studies* (Boston: Little, Brown, 1973).
[11] Gusfield, *op. cit.*, p. 8.

in politics. These people include not only office holders, but also those to whom they are most attentive and whose views they are most likely to know. Verba and Nie have found that the policy agendas of community leaders tend to correspond most closely with the views of the politically most active segments of the community. This correspondence, they suggest, is attributable largely to differential rates of participation rather than similarities in social background or interests. Political participation serves as a vehicle both for communicating information to government officials and for sanctioning those who fail to listen. Thus, we would expect governmental responsiveness in the sense of correspondence between the systemic and formal agendas to vary with scope and intensity of popular political involvement. Indeed, this is precisely the pattern that Verba and Nie find in their study of participation in sixty-four American communities.[12]

The narrower and more insulated the active participants in formulating the governmental agenda, the greater the gap between the formal and systemic agenda is likely to be. The complexity of government and diversity of its concerns tend to insulate many of its activities from widespread public scrutiny, even though they are nominally matters of public record. As a consequence, much of the governmental agenda is likely to be built without active participation and even knowledge on the part of most members of the general public. The dangers inherent in such limited and selective participation are mitigated in part by what Mayhew has called the "election connection." [13] Numerous studies have shown that elections do, in fact, create important incentives for office holders to attempt to minimize the gap between the formal and systemic agendas both by responding to popular preferences and by anticipating the public reactions to prospective agenda items.[14] The degree of accountability that elec-

---

[12] Sidney Verba and Norman Nie, *Participation in America* (New York: Harper & Row, 1972), pp. 299–333.

[13] David Mayhew, *Congress: The Electoral Connection* (New Haven: Yale University Press, 1974).

[14] See, for example, Susan B. Hansen, "Participation, Political Structure and Concurrence," *American Political Science Review* 69 (1975), pp. 1181–99; James Kuklinski, "Representativeness and Elections: A Policy Analysis," *American Political Science Review* 72 (1978), p. 174; and Bruce Cavala and Aaron Wildavsky, "The Political Feasibility of Income by Right," *Public Policy* 17 (1970), pp. 321–54.

tions afford is enhanced by the extent to which they are structured around political parties. Because government is a collective enterprise involving many decision-makers, individual office holders are likely to have only limited control over the governmental agenda and can hardly be held responsible for its contents. Parties, on the other hand, allow a large number of office holders to be held collectively responsible and thus facilitate more meaningful accountability of the government to the electorate.[15]

As important as they are, elections themselves are still rather blunt instruments for influencing the governmental agenda. Election campaigns do afford candidates an opportunity to influence the public agenda and through it the governmental agenda in more specific ways. Because of the media attention they come to command, candidates for major offices are often in a propitious position to call attention to an issue and influence its definition. Once in office, public officials are commonly expected to continue to participate actively in molding the public agenda, as well as to play a role in formulating the formal agenda of government. In the course of monitoring and helping to interpret public problems, they help to shape the very demands that are made upon themselves and others in government. Often office holders become prominent advocates of particular problems, problem definitions, or solutions. Their motives in doing so may be simply to satisfy the role expectations associated with their offices or to promote personal policy preferences. Often they are also motivated, at least in part, by a desire for reelection or higher office. Through conspicuous advocacy, they can build supportive constituencies that may be instrumental to these goals. Walker suggests that U.S. Senators, particularly those with presidential aspirations, frequently seek out issues to champion that can readily be defined as having broad social significance and are easily explained, issues like automobile, occupational, and coal mine safety.[16]

In American national politics, the President, of course, tends to be, and is expected to be, the primary articulator of major public problems. The issues that a President chooses to emphasize command almost automatic standing on the Congressional agenda. However,

---

[15] Hansen, *op. cit.*; and Everett Ladd, *Where Have All the Voters Gone?* (New York: Norton, 1982).

[16] Jack Walker, "Setting the Agenda for the U.S. Senate," *British Journal of Political Science* 7 (1977), pp. 432–45.

many of the policy initiatives of a President do not originate with him or even with the executive branch. Light finds that in formulating the President's domestic agenda, "issues are selected on the basis of perceived benefits [to the President]. . . . Presidents are quite willing to coopt ideas from any available source and . . . the campaigns and primaries are not significant institutional constraints on the agenda ideas." [17] Most of a President's major policy initiatives will revolve around issues that have achieved systemic agenda standing either prior to his picking them up or through his own advocacy prior to submitting them. In fact, the President's ability to exploit or mobilize public concern is perhaps his most powerful asset in assuring active consideration of an issue. In the absence of such concern, even presidential initiatives may receive little more than *pro forma* attention.

Presumptive Rights and Problem Ownership

By virtue of the offices they hold, Presidents and other office holders tend to enjoy a presumptive right to play a leading role in identifying and defining the problems that will command governmental attention. The scope of this presumption depends upon the office held and tends to be much broader for the President than for other public officials. Nonetheless, public asquiescence to, or acceptance of, such presumptive rights affords office holders substantial leverage in conflicts over the definition of an issue. Office holders, however, are not the only ones to enjoy such presumptive rights. They are also accorded to others who, by virtue of their positions, experiences, or presumed expertise, are assumed to have superior knowledge or understanding of particular types of problems and their solution possibilities. Gusfield refers to this as "ownership of public problems," suggesting that, like property ownership, it involves "attributes of control, exclusiveness, transferability, and potential loss." [18] Ownership in this sense, however, is more like a public trust. It is based on the attribution of authority and a willingness of people to defer to the judgments of others. It is always conditional and potentially subject to challenge and change.

[17] Paul Light, *The President's Agenda* (Baltimore: Johns Hopkins University Press, 1981), p. 11.
[18] Gusfield, *op. cit.*, p. 10.

A notable example is the presumptive right commonly accorded the medical profession and the medical service delivery bureaucracy to define the problems of health care policy in the United States. Alford suggests that the dominance of these groups, sustained by their "ownership" of problems in the area, have not only stifled reform but have contributed to the escalating costs of health care.[19] Over the last several decades, the scope of the medical profession's ownership of public problems has expanded. More and more problems have come to be defined as matters of individual pathology and thus "medical problems." As a consequence, the medical profession has gained at least partial ownership of problems in a wide variety of areas—e.g., mental health, aging, alcohol and substance abuse—that were once considered to be the province of others, namely, the family, the church, and law enforcement officials. Despite the competitive advantage that the medical profession enjoys in defining a variety of public problems, their authority in this regard is not beyond challenge. In the late 1970's, for example, a heated controversy developed over the legalization of the drug Laetrile, an alleged cure for cancer. Although the medical profession dismissed it as worthless and potentially dangerous, proponents of the drug's legalization succeeded in controlling the definition of the issue in at least some states. They did so by defining it as a matter of individual rights and freedom of choice.

Presumptive rights rest on a willingness of people to defer to some and not others in the framing of policy problems. They arise largely from commonly shared values and beliefs regarding the realities of social life and the appropriate division of labor in society. They are predicated not only on assumptions about the state of knowledge and who possesses it but also on past practices and established precedents for accommodating competing interests in society. In this sense, presumptive rights are the product of culturally accepted standards of procedural and substantive legitimacy. These standards define the prevailing public philosophy and serve to rationalize and justify the exercise of political power. Lowi suggests that since the 1930's, the American public philosophy has been based on a vulgarized version of pluralist theory, which he calls "interest group

---

[19] Robert Alford, *Health Care Politics* (Chicago: University of Chicago Press, 1975).

liberalism." [20] In effect, it sanctions a prominent role for major organized interests in defining those issues in which they have a stake.

The presence of such presumptive rights, be they based on interest or expertise, serves to structure participation in the agenda-
building process. These patterns tend to become institutionalized as
government organizes its activities around previously established
conceptions of problems warranting its attention and as consideration
of issues in these problem areas become routinized. Thus, "many
areas of policy tend to be dominated by a limited and relatively stable
set of actors operating within a relatively closed communications
network."[21] These actors constitute what is commonly called a policy
subsystem or subgovernment. At the national level, such subsystems
are typically composed of an executive agency, members of relevant
Congressional committees and subcommittees, and representatives of
major organized interests.[22] Derthick provides a detailed account of
one of these subsystems in her study of social security policy-making.
She finds that for years the governmental agenda in this area was
dominated by key executives in the Social Security Administration,
the chairman of the House Ways and Means Committee, and representatives of organized labor.[23]

Although they are sometimes called "iron triangles," most subsystems are neither so tightly structured nor as impenetrable as this
imagery suggests.[24] Nonetheless, subsystem participants tend to share
a common perspective on what is and is not problematic and on how
those problems should be defined. This is reflected in a specialized
and often arcane language peculiar to the policy area. While this
specialized language may facilitate communications within the sub-

[20] Theodore Lowi, "The Public Philosophy: Interest Group Liberalism,"
American Political Science Review 61 (1967), pp. 5–24.

[21] Roger W. Cobb and Charles D. Elder, "Communication and Public Policy,"
in Dan Nimmo and Keith Sanders (eds.), *Handbook of Political Communication* (Beverly Hills, Cal.: Sage Publications, 1981), p. 408.

[22] See Randall Ripley and Grace Franklin, *Congress, the Bureaucracy and
Public Policy* (Homewood, Ill.: Dorsey, 1980).

[23] Martha Derthick, *Policymaking for Social Security* (Washington, D.C.:
Brookings Institution, 1979).

[24] See Hugh Heclo, "Issue Networks and the Executive Establishment," in
Anthony King (ed.), *The New American Political System* (Washington, D.C.:
American Enterprise Institute, 1978); and James Wilson, "The Politics of
Regulation," in James Wilson (ed.), *The Politics of Regulation* (New York:
Basic Books, 1980).

system, it also renders much of the debate unintelligible to outsiders and acts as a barrier to broader participation in problem definition. In effect, it allows virtually all issues in an area to be defined as technical ones, as matters best left to the experts. It thus serves to insulate the subsystem from outside influence and helps to preserve the prevailing mobilization of bias in the policy area.

In the absence of a crisis, scandal, or major shift in leadership, policy subsystems are likely to exercise fairly exclusive control over what appears on the institutional agenda in their issue area and to do so without arousing or needing to arouse much public concern. Over time, the relative insulation of subsystem politics can contribute to a growing disparity between the systemic and formal agendas. As this becomes clear, the role of government, as well as what it attends to, may be called into question and become itself an issue on the systemic agenda. Indeed, this seems to have happened in the 1970's, fostering a climate of opinion receptive to Ronald Reagan's contention that "government was the problem" and paving the way for his election in 1980 on the promise of "getting government off people's backs."

It is probably the case that a major portion of the federal agenda is determined through subsystem politics. However, these subsystems are not likely to account for major policy innovations or policy changes. Although, over time, the cumulative impact of initiatives arising from a subsystem can be substantial, for the most part these initiatives tend to be incremental modifications or additions to existing policies. They tend to be constrained both by the established biases of the subsystem in terms of problem definition and by a desire to avoid disrupting existing accommodations among interests inside and outside of the subsystem.

Overcoming Systemic Biases

As we have repeatedly seen, control over the definition of what is at issue is a major determinant of success in the agenda-building process. There is a multiplicity of obstacles to gaining the active attention of government for new problems or definitions of problems. These include preexisting and often institutionalized biases that tend to force policy questions into established niches. Problems or problem definitions that do not fit into these niches are often ignored. This may be understood in part as a product of the existence of vested interest and the competitive advantage of some over others. Certainly, established interests can be expected to resist initiatives that may affect them adversely. However, more than this is involved.

The governmental agenda is always crowded, and there are always more matters competing for attention than can be actively considered. To make their job more manageable, policy-makers understandably attempt to reduce the potential uncertainties with which they must cope by structuring the process as much as possible. A lack of clarity regarding what is at issue and conflict over its definition create uncertainties and highlight risks that militate against formal consideration. These uncertainties are compounded by the fact that issue conflicts tend to revolve around not only the definition of the problem but also the feasibility of the solutions implied and the desirability and appropriateness of government involvement.

Lacking previously established access to the formal agenda and, in the case of redefinition of old issues, challenging institutionalized understandings of an issue area, new issues or major redefinitions of old ones thus tend to face formidable obstacles in gaining standing on the governmental agenda. These obstacles are likely to be overcome only through the mobilization of popular concern and the elevation of the issue to systemic agenda status. Jones provides a striking example of this in his study of the 1970 amendments to the Clean Air Act. He finds that perceived popular concern prompted major policy innovation with respect to air pollution, despite the resistance of powerful organized interests and the uncertain feasibility of the solutions involved.[25] Walker suggests that similar dynamics were involved in bringing motor vehicle safety standards to the top of the legislative agenda in the mid-1960's. Through aggressive public advocacy, proponents succeeded in shifting the frame of reference used in defining the problems of traffic safety from one focusing almost exclusively on driver performance to one emphasizing the design and safety characteristics of the automobile itself.[26] In his study of nonincremental

---

[25] Charles Jones, *Clean Air* (Pittsburgh: University of Pittsburgh Press, 1975).
[26] Jack Walker, "The Diffusion of Knowledge and Policy Change: Toward a Theory of Agenda Setting," paper delivered at the Annual Meeting of the American Political Science Association, August 29–September 2, 1974, Chicago, Illinois, pp. 25–27.

policy initiatives, Schulman also finds that success tends to hinge on the mobilization and maintenance of a supportive climate of public opinion.[27]

Because most people are not vigilant in monitoring the political process, mobilizing sufficient public support to command the active attention of government is no mean task. Conflicts and dramatic events may help to attract public attention; but unless they are effectively exploited, such happenings are not by themselves likely to galvanize opinion around an issue. Effective advocacy is needed. This task falls to people who are willing to invest their time and energy in promoting the issue. In chapter 5, we identified these people as initiators. These people represent one of two types of entrepreneurial roles that Eyestone suggests are critical in bringing about major policy innovations, the other being brokers. Initiators are instrumental in building public support and shepherding an idea to the governmental agenda; brokers act to see an idea through the maze of institutional processes necessary for its adoption as policy.[28] Both roles involve substantial commitment and are sometimes played by the same person.

Policy entrepreneurs are found both inside and outside of government. As we previously noted, elected officials frequently assume such roles. Nonelected officials also sometimes act as prime movers in promoting policy innovation. Outside of government, the exploits of people like Ralph Nader and John Gardner are well known. There are, however, countless others—people like Mary Lasker, who played a critical role in the creation of the National Institute on Cancer; Lois Gibbs, a Love Canal housewife whose untiring efforts helped to bring the problems of toxic waste into national focus; and Howard Jarvis and Paul Gann, who authored the California ballot initiative, Proposition 13, that sparked something of a nationwide tax revolt.

Of course, the mobilization of popular concerns does not assure that an issue will be acted upon or even seriously considered as a matter of public policy. Public concern is often short-lived and seems to follow an "issue attention cycle," as described by Downs.[29] None-

[27] Paul Schulman, *Large Scale Policy Making* (New York: Elsevier, 1980).
[28] Robert Eyestone, *From Social Issues to Public Policy* (New York: John Wiley, 1978), pp. 88–96.
[29] Anthony Downs, "Up and Down with Ecology—The Issue Attention Cycle," *Public Interest* 12 (1972), pp. 38–50.

theless, if effectively exploited, public concern creates enormous pressure that policy-makers are not likely to ignore if a compelling alternative is available.

The Changing Context of Agenda-Building

The content and dynamics of agenda-building are necessarily a function of the larger social, political, and economic context in which this process is embedded. That context is constantly changing, creating new constraints and altering old ones. Over the past two decades, for example, there have been many changes in the context of agenda-building in the United States. Not only has the scope of governmental activity increased enormously, but, spurred by the emphasis that the culture places on rationality and efficiency, there has been a marked trend toward the professionalization and bureaucratization of the policy process. Even agenda-building, perhaps the most quintessentially political aspect of the policy process has not escaped this drive toward ratiocination. As a consequence, more and more areas of policy have tended to become more exclusively the province of what Heclo calls "issue network" [30] and Walker refers to as "communities of policy professionals." [31] This has contributed to growing knowledge gaps that not only limit participation but render both the process and its product less intelligible to the general public.[32] This, in turn, has undoubtedly contributed to diminished popular confidence in government.

The development of mass media that are truly national in scope and communications technologies that allow members of the public to be reached both directly and selectively has also had profound effects on the agenda-building process.[33] Modern communication capabilities have contributed to a continuing individualization of American politics and to a declining reliance on traditional intermediate institutions such as groups and parties that once served to structure people's relationships to the larger polity. As a consequence,

[30] Heclo, *op. cit.*
[31] Walker, "The Diffusion of Knowledge," *op. cit.*
[32] Philip Tichenor, George Donohoe, and Clarice Olien, *Community Conflict and the Press* (Beverly Hills, Cal.: Sage Publications, 1980), p. 188.
[33] Cobb and Elder, *op. cit.*

American politics has become more fragmented and volatile. Elections have become more a vehicle for reflecting diversity than for aggregating it. Candidates and office holders have found it electorally more expeditious to go it alone than to support the development and maintenance of broad-based policy coalitions. Since policy is ultimately a collective endeavor, this makes it difficult to hold anyone accountable for what government does and does not do.

Modern communications have also facilitated the emergence of potent new groups led by issue entrepreneurs and organized around issues and ideas rather than economic and regional interests. Spurning the traditional norms of group politics, these groups have injected new problems and problem definitions into the policy process. They have often served as an effective counterforce to traditional economic interests, undermining cozy relationships and altering the prevailing biases in policy areas once thought immune to the mobilization of popular sentiment.[34] However, because of the expressive nature of the involvement of their adherents, these groups are potentially unstable. Moreover, because the people involved tend to be atypical in the intensity and extremity of their views, the very effectivenss of these groups can skew governmental policy away from the modal preferences of the general public.[35]

Actions of government and its expanding scope have also altered the content and dynamics of the agenda-building process both by altering the realities of social and political life and by fostering heightened expectations. Political reforms aimed at making political campaigns more democratic have contributed to the weakening of political parties and spawned a proliferation of political action committees promoting particularized interests.[36] Congressional reforms designed to make it a more democratic institution have further diffused legislative power and fragmented policy decision-making, enhancing the relative power of the bureaucracy and interest groups.[37] As the role of the federal government has expanded to include many of the traditional concerns of state and local government, these governments have increasingly assumed a role in national politics similar

---

[34] Wilson, *op. cit.*
[35] Verba and Nie, *op. cit.*, pp. 341–42.
[36] Ladd, *op. cit.*
[37] Larry Dodd and Richard Schott, *Congress and the Administrative State* (New York: John Wiley, 1979).

to that of other interest groups. Substantive and procedural policies pursued by government at all levels have frequently had unanticipated consequences and spillover effects that created new problems requiring attention. In this sense, policy has tended to become more and more its own cause.[38]

These changes and many others have served to alter the prevailing biases in American politics in a variety of ways. They have increased the flow of information nominally available to the public, but it is ever more specialized information. They have fostered the emergence of new groups and actors in the political process but at the same time have undermined traditional structures that have served to make that process comprehensible to the average citizen. They have opened up new opportunities for citizens participation, but they have not necessarily made the governmental agenda more responsive to the general public. In many ways, they have tended simply to further advantage the already advantaged and to frustrate the many for whom participation is a right and civic duty but not a consuming passion nor a full-time occupation.

---

[38] Wildavsky, *op. cit.*

Index